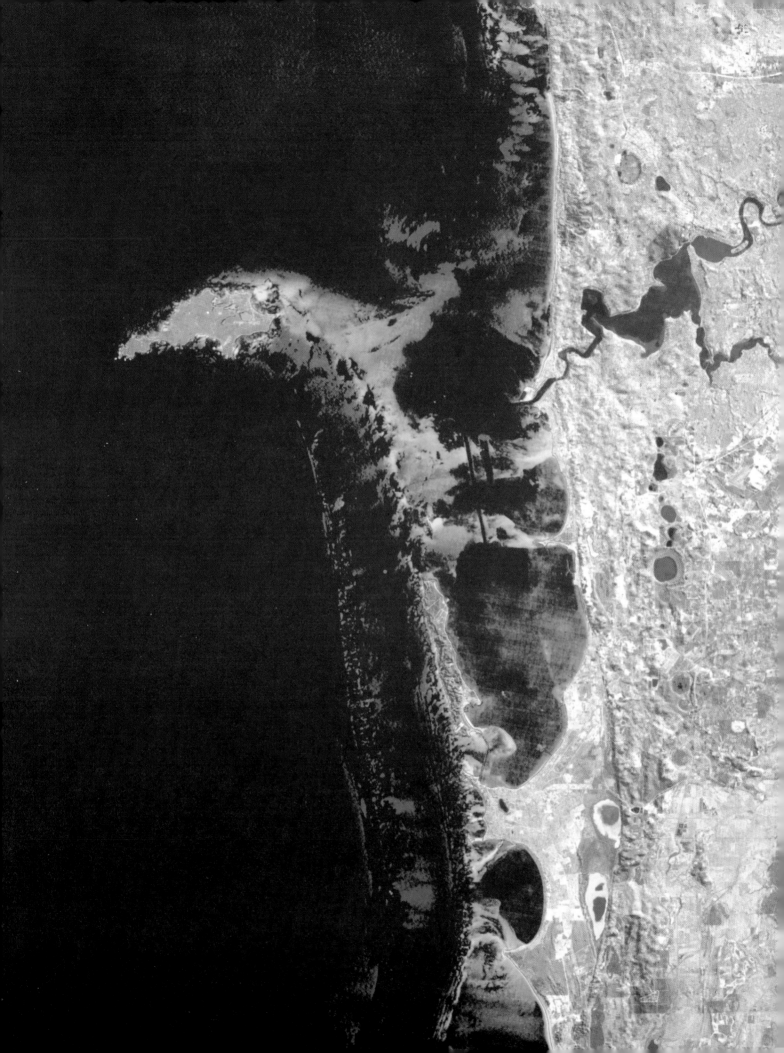

Donaldson + Warn Crossing Midfield

Geoffrey London and Duncan Richards

Birkhäuser – Publishers for Architecture Basel • Berlin • Boston   Foreword by Leon Van Schaik

A CIP catalogue record for this book is available from the Library of Congress, Washington D.C., USA

Die Deutsche Bibliothek - CIP-Einheitsaufnahme

Donaldson + Warn : Crossing Midfield. - Basel ; Berlin ; Boston : Birkhäuser, 2000
ISBN 3-7643-6334-7

© 2000 Birkhäuser – Publishers for Architecture, P.O.Box 133, CH-4010 Basel, Switzerland
Printed on acid-free paper produced from chlorine-free pulp. TCF ∞

Layout and cover design: Ray Leeves, Perth, Western Australia

Printed in Germany

ISBN 3-7643-6334-7

9 8 7 6 5 4 3 2 1

Thanks
Bill Busfield, Geoffrey London, Duncan Richards, Leon Van Schaik, Peter Parkinson, John Sunderland, Peter Kernot: for years of support and encouragement.
Ria Stein, editor at Birkhäuser, for her positive assistance.
Ray Leeves for his graphic design and questioning process.

This book is dedicated to our families and friends.

Foreword
Leon Van Schaik

Tension between the actual and the general tears through every aspect of life. Our understanding of the universe, heightened by a night staring at the stars, finds little to sustain it in the mundane act of driving back into the city limits after this experience of the sublime. We come to seek in architecture that connection between our spiritual awareness and our needs. This I feel is how architecture transforms building. Architecture is the art of translating ideals into form; in architecture the artefact realises the idea that gave it birth.

The levels of congruence between idea and form evident in the work of Donaldson + Warn led to the invitation to participate in RMIT (Royal Melbourne Institute of Technology) University's 'living legends' masters program. In this their work has been exposed to their peers and to national and international critics in a structured discourse over a period of three years. It is from this vantage point that I comment on their work, an important manœuvre in the evolution of Australian architecture, especially on the west coast.

The central text of this monograph spells out an involvement by Donaldson + Warn with the modern through Archigram and their mentors the Smithsons, and with Southern Californian architects. Indeed, taking an interest in the work of Donaldson + Warn may stem from a commitment to modernism, and a desire to describe its development wherever it can be found. There is a romance in observing, even in promoting, the idea that works conducted so far from the metropolises of modernity reveal in their distortions much that is concealed by a central orthodoxy. What indeed survives the transmission to such remoteness must be the most robust part of the tradition.

The central text suggests that Donaldson + Warn relate to a metropolitan discourse through these connections rather than to a discourse enchained to local heroes on either seaboard of Australia. Playing on the Wing of Pragmatism, Warn's RMIT University masters dissertation about the conditions of their practice also focuses on an American tradition rather than on the Australian development of utilitarian thinking which was this country's settlement thesis.

It is in this that I see two tendencies emerging, tendencies that will determine where they take their practice next. The first is the developing connection between their intellectual position and the form of their work. The second is an emerging confidence in their ability to co-opt and comment on the traditional forms of settlement that are described in the text, and that have become the local paradigm for the 'beautiful'.

Donaldson + Warn locate the theoretical basis of their work within the frame of pragmatism, a focus on the factual and on the technical, 'facing forward rather than upward', as Richard Rorty described protagonists philosopher and educator John Dewey and poet Walt Whitman. Warn argues that pragmatism deals with the dilemma in modernism's recurrent commitment to beauty (now so evident in neo-modernism) and what T.J. Clarke describes as its simultaneous discovery that the beautiful is 'nothing but mechanism, nothing but matter dictating (dead) form'. (L. Rainey, London Review of Books, 20 January 2000).

Pragmatism takes all of human experience, technical and poetic alike, coolly into account. This broad definition of what is included in the discourse of architectural practice seeks to ensure that more than the strictly utilitarian is considered in the process of defining and developing a design. Warn argues that by considering the effects and experiences of design decisions during a process built around a search to see what sequences of experience follow from an action or an idea, pragmatism can accommodate architecture's distinguishing need of functional purpose and practical outcomes while including more subjective values. This aligns with Rorty's description (London Review of Books, 16 March 2000) of Gadamer's, 'fusion of horizons', the argument that the intellectual must acknowledge all surrounding knowledge when working within the confines of a discipline.

The work of architecture, approached in this way, is thus the record of the intellectual endeavour that has brought it into being and of its context. Architecture is not the configuration of needs to conform to an aesthetic of received, international, taste.

The social ideals of modernism continued after the adoption of the ideology of the market in the Anglophone world through the concept of the Case Study – an exemplary work that could influence the wider context. The schools designed by the practice, such as the Ballajura Community College, push well beyond the formulae of the Department of Education to posit a rounded didactic environment. This work invites the lay public to make connections between an enriched architecture and their own wellbeing. Warn's working of Pragmatism into the processes of practice promises to deepen a dialogue between the work and the popular imagination that, if successful, could in turn diminish the anomie of those architecturally ambitious.

Many architects have taken a path of least resistance in relation to the popular imagination, bowing to market forces and giving what is assumed to be wanted. A public building culture consisting of inflated hipped, gabled and tiled project homes has resulted from this reluctance to take people beyond their immediate experience.

Much of the search for second order modernism in architecture around the world has the sentimentality of a merely stylistic return to the minimalist or 'existenzminimum' concerns of the first half of the century. But there is a deeper re-investigation of that heritage under way in Perth, and in this I think the houses of Donaldson + Warn are also significant. The houses of Donaldson + Warn are deliberate case studies. They have re-established the courtyard house as a viable type for denser urban situations or sub-divisions (Chauvel House, Lincoln St Duplex). They have explored oppositions between massive rammed earth construction and framed construction, re-articulating the way in which micro-climates are acknowledged and capitalised upon (Goddard House).

Without pandering to market assumptions, Donaldson + Warn have found it possible to reconstitute traditional forms into a new composition, as I have argued in a review of the Glick House for Monument (Issue 32, October/November 1999). In this house the traditional plan of the terrace house is reorganised through three stories. But they do so in such a manner that they engage head on with 'the deep ludicrousness of the lyric' (L. Rainey) that does seem to be the prevailing idea of beauty in suburban Perth. Pragmatism, as they employ it, enables them to avoid the simple opposition of received suburban form and "high art...depictions of beauty commonly manifest in the aesthetics of minimalism..." (G. Warn).

What makes comparisons between the work of Donaldson + Warn and USA west coast architect Eames poignant is their alignment with the ideals that drove that work, even when so removed in time. Despite the tide of development that seems to ignore experimental refinement of what is good and possible, they persist, as did Eames, in their determination to demonstrate how things could be better. This is an approach that is being explored across Australia. Architects examine the self-made fibro houses that are endemic on the Australian coast. They adopt the same technology. They then marshal these elements into a higher order that renders them conscious works of architecture. They know that Surfurbia is not reached head on, but by stealth.

Their most developed work respects the actual and the ideal, and it marshals the connections between the easy lyricism of the place and its possible, nobler human futures. This is the point of hope to which the work of Donaldson + Warn brings us on the west coast, a coast which holds for Australia, as did the west coast of the USA, the hope of transcending the lyrical and the utilitarian.

Previous page: City carpark staircase, Perth Cultural Centre. Facing page: Surfer, City Beach Perth Western Australia

The cool side

This family home, built on a former truck depot, was commissioned by a couple who own a contemporary art gallery. Construed as a linear form with a strong counter-axis, the house is a play of binary opposites; warm and cool, sunny and shady, in and out, up and down, metal and masonry, dry and wet, industrial fabrication and craft construction, building and garden, heavy and light, etc. Tight formalism was intentionally loosened by and for subjective idiosyncrasies. ✚ The house was constructed by the owners who enlisted help from several of their artist friends. This condition encouraged us to hold open the conventional delivery process to allow for local interpretation and modifications of the design in response to construction skills and methods, time, money and the flow of new inspirations. ✚ Located close to one boundary the house divides the site into a sunny and warm walled garden and a narrow, cool court. The long feature wall that dominates the northern façade is made from crushed limestone rock, a local stone, mixed with coloured sands and cement. The mix is 'rammed' into timber forms and is set in linear runs. The opposite side of the house is fabricated from lightweight framing and clad in galvanised corrugated steel sheet. Rammed earth and corrugated steel were common building materials used by the early European settlers, albeit in a different style to this residence. ✚ Sliding glazed doors and open planning on the ground floor enable cross ventilation and easy transgression between interior and exterior. Simple furniture and splendid artworks animate the rectangular geometry of the interior spaces. The resulting home is spacious and welcoming with a relaxed and easy atmosphere.

Dining space and kitchen beyond. Linear artwork above kitchen by Yurek Wybràniec and Daniel Götten

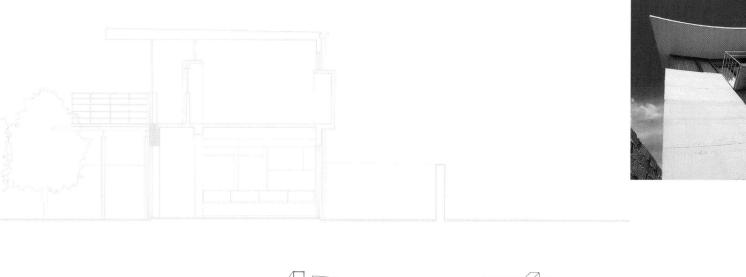

North

East

South

Study elevations

West

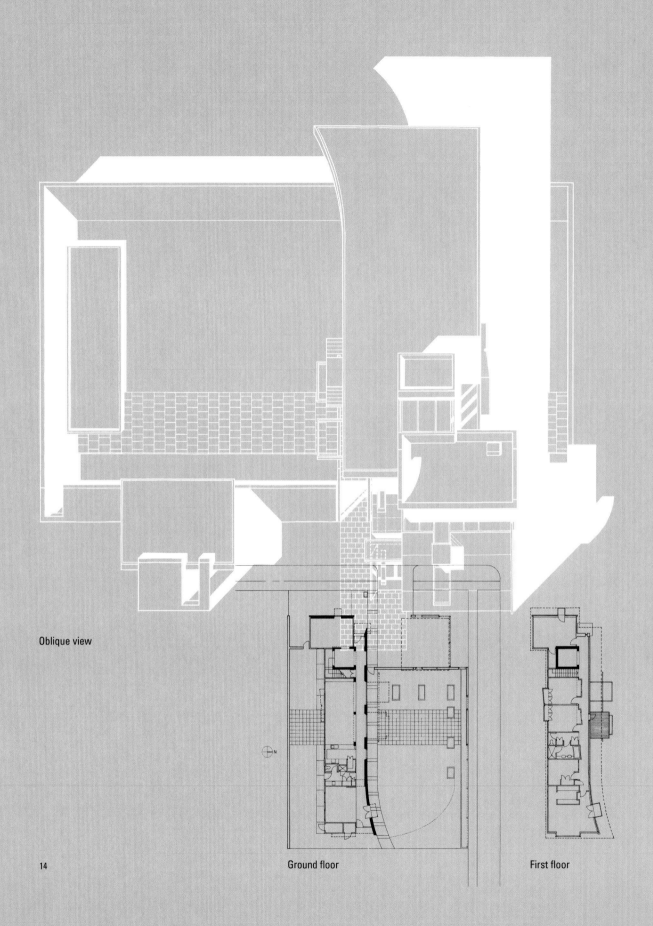

Oblique view

Ground floor

First floor

First floor corridor looking east, towards main bedroom

Donaldson+Warn Operating on the Edge

Geoffrey London Duncan Richards

Donaldson + Warn – Operating on the Edge

Introduction

Perth, the capital of Western Australia, is a city that always seems to be sliding off the edges of the horizon. There is a dominating sense of convex rather than concave space, opening the city up to a vast sky and relentless glare from the sun. Perth is an isolated oasis sandwiched between the desert and the Indian Ocean, an exotic new settlement grafted onto the ancient land of aboriginal occupation, the only major centre of population for a distance of several hours by aeroplane. Even today, to leave the city by car is to become very quickly aware of a vast unpopulated inland.

It is a linear city stretching out along a north-south 60 kilometre freeway following the flat scrubby coast, clinging to contact with the sea. From the air, it is an endless suburban mat studded with the blue of swimming pools, a depopulated urban centre set on a wide river system. It is a singularly hedonistic city with an enviably high standard of living, eternal blue skies, and a hot Mediterranean climate.

Since its settlement by the British as the far-flung Swan River Colony in 1829, Perth architecture has been characterised by attempts to transplant building forms from elsewhere and their adaptation to local conditions. Perth has had two major spurts of building growth, both linked to significant mineral discoveries. The first was the Western Australian gold rush of the 1890s with its associated rush of architects migrating to Perth from Britain and the eastern cities of Australia, correctly anticipating a building boom. This resulted in the extensive rebuilding of Perth and its port, Fremantle, and in a fine collection of ebullient new buildings confidently displaying a wide range of stylistic sources. Emerging from the mix of Arts and Crafts, Classical revivalism, Gothic revivalism and their eclectic variants, was an interest in applying these styles to the particular conditions of Perth. The second mining boom occurred in the 1960s and early 1970s. The boom, this time in iron ore and nickel, resulted in large tracts of the city of Perth being substantially rebuilt as a way of proclaiming the new found wealth, and the subsequent loss of a number of buildings spanning a rich variety of architectural styles. They were replaced, in the main, by undistinguished internationalist buildings with little regard for local factors. Perth's ongoing rebuilding of itself emphasises the precariousness of its grip on the edge of this ancient place, heightening the contrast between the ever-'newness' of the city and the awesomely old land.

Although now a city of one and a half million people, Perth does not have a significant urban tradition. From the outset the city centre was subdivided into a collection of residential blocks establishing the framework for a non-urban, a sub-urban condition. It is a city with significantly greater emphasis on building the private realm of the suburb than on the public realm of the urban centre. The public realm is now most often located in suburban shopping malls or in nature: the beaches, the parks, the river, rather than in the built forms of a city centre. There has been an unwillingness to make a substantial investment in the architecture of the public realm. This results in a society that has little exposure to and therefore little understanding of the potential of public architecture to help form the local culture.

Even with the benefit of rapid air transport and virtually instantaneous electronic communications for residents and visitors, the city of Perth continues to seem isolated and remote, one of the world's last frontiers. Such isolation can create freedom from, or ignorance of, the cultural imperatives of the time: it can allow the possibility of creative re-readings or mis-readings of ideas transmitted by way of word or image from elsewhere. There is also the possibility of narrowness of thinking, a short sighted frontier mode of decision making characterised by a lack of historical perspective, an absence of ideals and a lack of commitment to the value of architecture. As the writer and cultural historian, Simon Leys, observes in his essay, 'The Paradox of Provincialism':

"The death of culture lies in self-centredness, self-sufficiency and isolation." [1]

The complexities and challenges of this set of circumstances are reflected in the work of Donaldson + Warn, a Perth architectural practice. The partners, Dick Donaldson and Geoff Warn, acknowledge that they are preoccupied with creating an architecture from the particular conditions of practising in Perth. Warn has posed the question:

"Can our work which emanates from within this local context – beyond the critical supervision of the established centres of culture – be forged into something of worth to a wider debate about the value of contemporary architecture to contemporary society?" [2]

After fifteen years in an architectural practice and a partnership dating back to student days, D+W's evolving and rigorous architectural project is, in response to Warn's own question and as presented in this essay, clearly able to contribute to this wider debate.

While D+W are concerned with the implications of producing what they call a 'localised architecture', from the start their work has shown a thoughtful tension arising from the relationship between the local and the universal. They have always maintained active links with the broader international community of architects and sustained a belief in the potential embodied in the ideals of early modernism. The modernist imperative to be 'progressive' and 'radical' is a difficult project in a cultural context often suspicious and sceptical of these orientations when applied to architecture. Although West Australians show a willingness to accept progress and constantly strive for the new and the better, this rarely emerges in its architecture. Instead, there is an insistent harking back to a nostalgic view of settlement, a desire to reproduce the forms of earlier occupation and the pioneering spirit they represent. D+W have consistently resisted the provincialism of conforming to what they regard as modest levels of local architectural expectations. Instead, they have attempted, intelligently and creatively, to form their own architectural response to the circumstances of their city.

And yet, to those architects in other parts of the world, used to working within the constraints of a powerful pre-existing architectural culture, the situation in Perth, Western Australia, could seem to offer a particular kind of freedom. As Simon Leys' paradox would have it:

"People who live in Paris, London or New York have a thousand convincing reasons to feel that they are 'where the action is', and therefore they tend to become oblivious of the fact that rich developments are also taking place elsewhere. This is something which educated people who live in a village are unlikely ever to forget." [3]

Background

Modern architecture in Western Australia developed almost independently of its growth in other parts of Australia. There was no school of architecture in Perth until after WWII and the new graduates from the Perth Technical College were strongly encouraged to gain international experience, almost always in England. Their education left them confident in their application of a version of modernism skewed towards the practical and towards the potential of local building conventions to be adapted to new formal possibilities. D+W, coming from an education shaped by the Perth Technical College, have followed a similar pattern. They are aware of the strengths of the architectural culture in other parts of Australia and laud the intense exchange of ideas about architecture there but, like their predecessors with their almost antagonistic architectural independence from the rest of Australia, don't seem to wish to take part in that conversation.

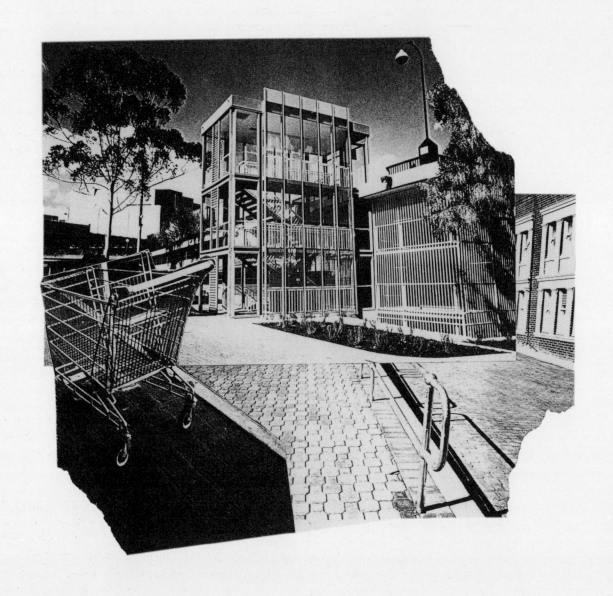

Drawing by Virginia Ward for a public artwork adjacent the city carpark staircase

Perhaps as a sign of affiliation with this local tradition, Geoff Warn chooses to live in a house in suburban Perth which dates from this period of modernism. These modernist houses, finely tuned to the local conditions, are a dwindling and widely unloved species, appreciated only by a small band of aficionados.

While D+W's buildings are also very local, their exemplars may be located in the traditional source of Perth modernism, England and, more directly, in leap-frogging the east coast of Australia and landing in California.

The architectural partnership of Dick Donaldson and Geoff Warn, while established in 1985, actually began in 1972 when, as switched-on lads from the suburbs of Perth, they initially met as first year students at the Western Australian Institute of Technology. They quickly became a unit, propelled by a common set of interests and a developing intensity and passion for the subject. Their design teacher, Bill Busfield, recollects an early project which focused on the design and making of large things. The first year students, D+W, chose to make a hot air balloon at one-third full size. They relentlessly pursued all aspects of the design, its materials, its sponsorship and its manufacture: the thoroughness and fanaticism of their exploration impressed Busfield enormously. In their final year they undertook a joint thesis which proposed environmental guidelines for beachside developments. This had much to say about their future interests, their edgy relationship to the place, and the desire to work together.

Bill Busfield had recently arrived in Perth after having taught at the Architectural Association School of Architecture in London and working there as an architect, most recently in the development of sophisticated cladding systems with the architectural firm of Pearson International. In addition to proving an effective teacher and motivator for the nascent partnership of D+W, he also provided an induction into another architectural world – that of late 1960s London, Archigram, and the promise of an unfettered technology. The mystique and exoticism of this world, with its own language, its own descriptive style, its own fantasy, was intoxicating for the first year students Donaldson and Warn. And integral to its ethos was an unwavering belief in the transforming power of the architect, as an instrument of social good, as the prophet ahead of his time, expecting, defiantly, to be unheeded.

Busfield was helpful in arranging architectural introductions for Warn when, after graduating, he went to live in London in 1977. He worked initially for Pearson International and then for the Farrell Grimshaw Partnership. After working for Loftus and Walker, a Perth architectural practice with a strong emphasis on the methodology of building construction, Donaldson also travelled this well-worn path of young Perth architects to London where he worked for the Goddard Manton Partnership. The obligatory path overseas has long been institutionalised by the Western Australian Chapter of the Royal Australian Institute of Architects with their most prestigious award to graduating architects being a travelling scholarship.

The experience in and exposure to London at this time has left an imprint on Donaldson and Warn's practice. There is a crankiness, an unwillingness to accept conventional solutions, a focus on how ideas generate buildings, a strong interest in the materiality and assembly of buildings, and the maintenance of a non-corporate office, all of which relates to the veil of influence left on London architecture of the time by Alison and Peter Smithson. Whilst in London, Dick Donaldson and Geoff Warn travelled independently on numerous architectural pilgrimages to Europe and subsequently to the USA, developing their critical repertoire and an international perspective.

In his 1971 book, 'Los Angeles: The Architecture of Four Ecologies,' Reyner Banham claimed that, 'Los Angeles is the greatest City-on-the-Shore in the world; its only notable rival, in fact, is Rio de Janeiro, and its only rival in *potential* is, probably, Perth, Western Australia.'[4] Banham made a brief visit to Perth in 1962 and saw the city with a perceptive outsider's eye, saw its comparative place in a contemporary global culture. The context, for Banham, was the virtues of the ecology of 'Surfurbia' and in making a crucial point regarding the exuberance, energy and innovation of the suburban west coast scene, he pointed out parallels between Los Angeles and Perth. As if in response to Banham's optimistic prediction, one of the most significant and fruitful connections that Geoff Warn has maintained over the years has been with the city of Los Angeles and with several architects who practice there. D+W have turned consistently to Los Angeles for direction and architectural impetus. What seems to be characteristic of the architects they admire in Los Angeles, in addition to their celebration of popular culture, is a witty, self-aware grasp of the interesting contradictions and ever shifting edges of their society and its built environment, issues that similarly engage D+W.

The Smithsons can again be cited as a source for this interest. From the middle of the 1950s they wrote numerous articles in 'Architectural Design' on the particularly modern virtues of Charles and Ray Eames. They described Charles Eames as a natural Californian man, using his native resources and know-how, of the film-making, the aircraft and the advertising industries, of shopping by the catalogue, of seeing the ordinary as magical and making art forms out of ordinary life.[5] The Smithsons recognised, before most, the critical and influential move by the Eames from the worlds of the painters into the world of the advertising layout men, into the world of the cinema eye and the production aircraft, while remaining with the 'magic of rectangle and repetition that was the gift of the thirties.'[6] The Smithsons' enthusiasm for the Eames' new version of modernism was carried to the students at the Western Australian Institute of Technology by Busfield and another lecturer there, Duncan Richards.

The Eames house in Santa Monica has a strangely familiar setting to an Australian, turned towards the sea and surrounded by expatriate eucalypts, described affectionately by Frank Lloyd Wright as 'tall tattered ladies', with their characteristic mottled light, sounds of rustling brittle leaves and bracing scent. It has a rare relentlessness of attitude and inventive rigour of technique that was not lost on D+W. The house can be seen as an encapsulation of many of the factors that proved attractive to them in Los Angeles. It was the most influential of the experimental houses in the Case Study Houses Program launched by John Entenza in 'Arts & Architecture', an exercise of great optimism and didactic social engagement for the architect. It developed an aesthetic based on the visibility of all the architectural elements and the inventive use of commonplace industrially produced materials. The framing and the skin of the pavilions was deft and refined while the extensive glazing of the separated pavilions admitted the benign climate and easy access to the site. D+W's early Chauvel House is, in many respects, a homage to the Eames house.

If the design issues explored by the Eames in their own house provided an initial take-off point and remain as an underlying armature of ideas for Donaldson + Warn, the early work of Frank Gehry, Coy Howard, Eric Moss, Jim Stafford, Thom Mayne and Michael Rotondi became the subsequent models. In his exacting manner, borne of a clear conviction in his own interests, Geoff Warn pursued and ferreted out Mayne and Rotondi in the formative years of Morphosis, living in their studio while working for them for a brief period. This was a time when Morphosis was designing buildings of extreme frugality, working with the challenge of trying to invent an architecture out of very little.

The Californian experience allowed Warn to build on an earlier interest in Americana nourished from the time he had carried the unlikely mantle of Western Australian yoyo champion, coupled with the focus of his generation on American beach culture, film, music and cars. The vitality of the American west coast was to be the magnet: the political awareness, urbanity, contemporary music scene and counter-culture of San Francisco proved alluring. But in Los Angeles, Warn, like Banham, recognised the city Perth might become – both cities as the brash west coast cousins to the larger cultural epicentres on the east coast; both cities blessed with a sea where the sun sets rather than rises, with endless superb beaches and a climate that allows their full appreciation. And, importantly, both were cities where everything appeared possible, arising from a frontier, edge-of-the-world mentality.

Morphosis developed an architecture of assemblage, of clearly defined and independent but connected elements. Their work reflected on architecture as a deliberately constructed reality in a particular time and place, and this aspect and its legibility provided a major formal impetus for them. It also prompted a way of working, of designing, that made the process visible and insisted on it being a major presence in the project. Their drawings and models carry with them the traces and residues of the testing, the connections and the mechanics.

Similarly, D+W make extensive use of exploded axonometrics and models displaying the constituent parts. They also have an interest in displaying the process of construction, in highlighting the placing of one element next to another and its form of connection, in layering and peeling back to expose. Dick Donaldson regards the layering in their work as a formal depiction of the building's conceptual organisation and process of assembly. The articulation of separate elements and the open expression of junctions also allows for their recurring interest in what they call 'loose fit':

"Related to the thoughts on planning composition and the discussion on detailing and finish is the idea of a 'loose fit' architecture. The loose and sometimes makeshift arrangement of parts and doubling-up of functions in a 'resourceful' and often temporary way seems to characterise much in the ongoing settlement of this State." [7]

To D+W this issue of 'loose fit' is important in other ways: they consider that without it the finished architecture is often diagrammatically explicit but without sufficient levels of engagement, and that a certain level of ambiguity is appropriate in a contemporary world without certainties.

There is an affiliation with Morphosis that may also be explained through the similarities in architectural education of the period which had a strong focus on a rational/scientific approach to meeting the quantifiable requirements of both program and environment. Like Morphosis there has been a gradual shedding by D+W of the learned necessity of a direct correlation between function and form and an embrace of the tectonic as a means of formal experimentation.

This point is developed by Dick Donaldson when he speaks of his admiration for Renzo Piano:

"I like his inventive approach to design and 'soft' sophisticated approach to technology [and] his interest in construction techniques and approach to prefabrication." [8]

While recognising all these sources and influences, D+W have developed their own architectural approach that relates very much to their location and to their attempts to match aspirations with an often indifferent reality.

They gain an almost perverse sustenance from seeing themselves as outsiders, as having concerns which separate them from the mainstream of architectural practice in Perth. As a result, they have generated their own self-contained satellite of architectural culture: it is built around a long-term commitment to teaching at the two schools of architecture in the city – teaching as an opportunity to explore, define and refine their own actions as well as an opportunity to speculate on ideas with students; to an office environment that attracts and nourishes bright young employees but nevertheless encourages their development elsewhere; to organising talks about current architectural issues; to maintaining an atelier-like office and resisting the corporatisation of their practice; and to sustaining a commitment to the progressive in architecture. And yet, defying their own sense of being unrecognised prophets, they have won numerous local architectural awards, demonstrating a level of recognition for their achievements that belies their self-image as the outsiders.

The maintenance of this self-image perhaps has more to do with a long-term identification with the avant-garde, an affiliation that Donaldson and Warn zealously and determinedly preserve. As part of this attitude they regard many of their projects as prototypes, as test pieces for a much grander architectural ambition. This helps explain the visionary strength of their Perth Foreshore Competition entry, the positing of the Lincoln Street houses as an alternative model to the suburban dream, and their almost obsessive desire for clarity of articulation – in building form and in its explication. They assume, without bombast, a didactic position – a passion to share their architectural commitment in a place where, frustratingly for them, such commitment is often not highly valued.

Because of this and because Perth is an isolated city on the edge of the world, many of the best young architectural graduates seek work in larger, more architecturally vital cities. There has been a conspicuous drain of talent from Perth, not only to the larger Australian cities of Melbourne and Sydney, but also to numerous centres of architectural activity in Europe, Asia, and the USA. But Donaldson and Warn, after their extended periods of work overseas, returned to Perth, started their own office, and have tenaciously stayed on. They are undoubtedly committed to their city and to pursuing an architecture that they regard as 'appropriate.' By this, they don't mean the search for some mystical and elusive 'spirit of place' but, rather, an adjustment of their aspirations in recognition of local modes of building and cultural expectations. They take the positive cast, seeking to make good work from limited ideas, limited materials and low budgets. One of their strategies is to focus the budget on a major element of the building rather than distributing it evenly across the project.

D+W maintain a commitment to selected early modernist ideals: they remain believers in a world that can be transformed into a better place with the help of architecture, and they retain a faith in the potential of technology to enable that transformation. In Perth their work is distinctive: it dogmatically asserts this heroic potential of architecture while, simultaneously, it often demonstrates a quirky vitality and originality. At times, because of the nature of the particular project, this can be recognised in small details, such as in the heavily worked entrances to the Large Animal Facility at The University of Western Australia, while at other times, such as at the Ballajura Community College, an almost nostalgic return to the belief in a holistic systematisation of architecture, has led to a building that is thoroughly saturated with this doctrine. As part of this belief in the transforming potential of architecture, D+W place great emphasis on carrying the client with them, on making the client aware of their process of reaching design decisions and including them in those decisions. They make many models and produce numerous explanatory diagrams to aid in fitting the building closely to clients' needs. The practice prides itself on extending and opening up the expectations of both clients and users, and on placing considerable focus on the experiential aspects of their buildings.

Themes and Projects

A particular condition of the city of Perth is that it is suburban, endlessly suburban. Its suburbs sprawl like few other cities and the dream of ownership of an individual house on an individual block of land seems to be more realised and more realisable in this city than just about anywhere else. All these suburbs have evolved without substantial involvement of architects.

And yet, traditionally, the best work of young architects in Australia is done in the suburbs through an early house commission. This was the case for Donaldson and Warn. The Chauvel house of 1988 was a particularly well-resolved early work in which the themes of their later work can be seen in their fledgling states. The house is formed by two crisply defined pavilions of thin walls comprised of white aluminium framed glass and western red cedar cladding boards. Concrete block is used for the service spine on the western side and for boundary walls. The juxtaposition of the emphatically solid and the light walls with their drummy box-like quality is assured and fully considered: the lightweight walls have a surprising thinness where you can read all the elements coming together with clarity at the corner. The two pavilions are linked by an expressionistic, almost alien, insert which arches over the kitchen on the ground floor and a bridge on the upper floor, joining the study to the parent's bedroom. The front pavilion contains a double volume space opening out to the courtyard which is defined by the two pavilions. This courtyard, the open room, has proved to be the centre of the house – it is critical for family interaction, light, contact with the elements and the filtering of views.

The manipulation of light has been a recurring source for the designs of Donaldson and Warn.

"Western Australia's strong and glaring sunlight enables us to delineate a building's perimeter and paint its facades with crisp, black shapes and dappled patterns that are forever moving. Various forms of canopies, screens and filters are used regularly to modify light in and around our designs." [9]

In the Chauvel house light is manipulated and controlled in a variety of ways: the devices that screen or shade or filter become major visual elements. They are reconstituted from the conventional elements of window hoods. Various means of filtering light are used: screens, moveable and fixed; textured and coloured glass; and perforated metal.

The house accommodates the best values of suburbia: space, air, garden, independence, but has a combativeness to it, a discomfort in the street, that suggests a subversive undertone: we're here but we're not a benign presence because we're going to challenge your aesthetic assumptions and your suburban values. D+W's work seems always to gravitate towards more urban models, towards proposing alternatives to the suburban hegemony. The Chauvel house could well be one of a row of linked terrace houses; it has the appearance of a house that was designed to be repeated, a prototype for more dense, more urban living, rather than a one-off independent suburban object. D+W's pursuit of the more public realm of the urban in a culture so committed to the private realm of the suburban again demonstrates their contrariness, their assumption of the role of the outsider, but it is also a productive tension within their way of working.

Two recent housing projects provide evidence of a developed approach to the inner suburb. The Glick house shows a willingness to take on the suburb – to be aggressive in its different-ness. It sits defiantly box-like on its site, surrounded by modest cottages built over a range of decades spanning the middle of the 20th century. The house has that element of surprise – that momentary hesitation – 'Oh, I didn't think that houses were like that.' With its engineering aesthetic it would be more at home in a light industrial estate than in its quiet inner suburban street.

One of the consistently interesting aspects of this project is the oddity of it, the perversities of certain design decisions, like the opposite pitching of the roof plane and the upper floor plane. The roof plane is overstated by being made ostentatiously thick and draining to a giant gutter. There is a purposefully 'clunky' quality to this building. It is a house and studio for a sculptor, with the studio on the ground floor, accessed from the street by wide doors concealed within the texture and pattern of the cladding. It provides a roof terrace, bracingly spartan and utilitarian with its concrete paving slabs and tubular steel scaffolding-like handrail – and you sit up there elevated above the suburb and you've got the vast sky. The provision of a roof deck is one of the great missed suburban opportunities in Perth, with the houses conventionally covered in heavy concrete or clay tiles.

Some key aspects of the building's form are determined by the meeting of restrictions placed by the local authority. For example, there was a requirement that the upper storey windows facing away from the street have a sufficiently high sill to restrict views into neighbours' back yards. This constraint has been turned into a positive design opportunity as that height becomes a kind of datum for a high strip of glazing wrapping around the whole building and lifting the roof from the walls. The lighting of this strip increases the sense of the huge floating roof and the drama of the building.

There is a Corbusian quality to the Glick house in its recognition of the heroic aspects of living – like the boxer boxing in the open volume of the apartments Le Corbusier designed for Edmond Wanner in 1928-9. It suggests that ordinary living is noble and sublime, that it isn't just a domestic operation, it's elevated beyond that: we're not here just for survival, we're here to celebrate the process. And in the rawness and toughness of the building there is an eschewing of the safe cloying comfort and complacency to be found in aspects of suburban living. This house touches on those heroic dimensions and is a quality of modernism that has rarely been explored in Perth.

The Lincoln Street duplex is located on the northern edge of the city centre. It offers the possibility of a new inner suburban housing type capable of considerable variational development, many permutations and combinations. Rather than an object sitting within a larger site, this duplex occupies the whole site, defining its limits with a wall, solid in parts and open elsewhere, acting as a filter for light, privacy and breezes. This wall is like a carapace within which the more vulnerable and private parts of the house nestle, a masonry frame in which the house is slung. Here, another theme of D+W, determined in part by location and climate, can be recognised: the blurring of edges between the inside and outside by making the external wall layered and eventful.

Like the Chauvel house, the duplex is in the form of a pair of two-storey pavilions, in this case separated by a courtyard with glazing at ground floor level that opens up entirely to create an outdoor room and floods light into the centre of the house. But unlike the Chauvel house, the link is not a habitable space, it is in the form of an extender, a ceremonial entrance and corridor, lending a sense of the theatrical to the house. Stretching the house in this manner also activates the potential of the loose fit sought by D+W, suggesting a variety of uses for the ground floor rooms and allowing considerable choice within the house type. The current occupants provide a picture book demonstration of its potential: on one side of the party wall the lower front rooms are used for a home office whereas on the other side they are used as a self-contained apartment for an elderly relative. The living room is placed upstairs and to the rear: an open glass box inflected through a tilted ceiling plane towards views of the near city, visually connecting the house to its nearby urban setting. Numerous suburban conventions are upturned in these planning strategies.

The pursuit of the urban by D+W is not limited to housing projects. The Lakeland High School challenged the prevailing layout of suburban schools that emphasised control, surveillance and ease of access, and which were built in the ubiquitous brick-and-tile of suburbia as a kind of big house. D+W reconfigured the conventional planning and adopted hierarchical urban ordering strategies with major and minor pathways and major and minor paved courtyards. Instead of the vast unshaded quadrangles and residual unplanned external spaces, their carefully designed and more intimate contained spaces, swelling at intersections of pathways or tucked in between buildings, would, they suggest, promote greater possibilities for human interaction and thus facilitate learning. The community aspects of the school were given greater architectural focus and the forms made less like the expanded domestic. Here, urban strategies are deployed in the suburbs with the aim of providing a superior setting for learning.

D+W have consistently attempted to propose a more urban future for Perth and at the same time, to encourage the pursuit of a greater architectural expectation from clients.

The 1991 Perth Foreshore Competition resulted in one of the practice's strongest and most important projects but one that can be seen to be a victim of a lack of political will. It was a defiant submission because it challenged the competition guidelines which inhibited the potential of the waterfront to be urban in any way that involved bringing buildings to the river. The city centre is currently separated from the river by a broad sweep of parklands and roadway. D+W introduced two major urban arms which had the potential to transform the city by crossing the east-west linear pattern of Perth, parallel to the river, and carrying the city across the parklands and down to the river. The western arm extends the area of civic and commercial facilities by taking its cue from an existing but relatively minor north-south axis. The second arm, to the east of the city centre, introduces a new area of major urban residential development. The primary objectives of their design were to bring the city directly to the water with a new civic heart and to attract a significantly greater residential population to the city. It was a deeply ambitious project in a competition where few other submissions demonstrated that level of urban ambition. It smacks of someone saying: 'What's really good for this city?', rather than, 'What do we need to do to win the competition?' And it comes out of: 'We live here, we know what this city is about and what it could be': local and not external influences generated the design. There is a substantial and coherent body of ideas underpinning the project. It showed the potential for an achievable urbanity and, importantly, a fruitful relationship between built form and nature, but the competition assessors and the government recoiled from it.

One project where such a relationship was able to develop fully was the winning competition entry for the Valley of the Giants Tree Top Walk, a collaborative exercise between the architects D+W, the sculptor David Jones, and the engineer Adrian Roberts from Ove Arup and Partners. This 600 metre walkway is suspended in a section of the awesome Tinglewood forest in the south-west of Western Australia and offers the visitor an unprecedented view of these giant trees. The inclined walkway is accessed at ground level but the ground quickly drops away to a deep valley leaving the walkway hoisted, spectacularly, over 40 metres above the valley floor. It comprises six lightweight trusses bridging between seven guyed pylons. The ideas for the structure grew directly from the local flora: the design of the pylons echoes the tassel flower with its strong fingers of petals, while the strength inherent in the form of sword grass underlies the truss design. The walkway is a transparent delicate structure that shudders intentionally with the action of walking. At the heights reached above the valley this is disconcerting and, according to the accompanying pamphlet, challenges 'the majority to extend their normal comfort zones.' It brings the visitor, through a cleverly conceived and resolved structure, into intimate contact with a rarely viewed aspect of nature – the tree canopies.

D+W are inextricably linked to their location as their work is forged by a combination of the battles they fight and the conditions they choose to work within. They continue to maintain their ambitions and aspirations in the face of the difficulties they recognise in producing architecture in Perth. Frustrations become converted into a positive twist:

"There seems to be a close relationship between the local context and the sense of incompleteness that characterises our projects. In more recent designs I have tried to utilise this condition as a working opportunity"[10]

The new Palandri Winery for the Margaret River Wine Production Company is an example of this approach. It uses a long wall of tilt-up concrete slabs acting both as a giant rural roadside billboard and as a division between the two aspects of its operation, the manufacturing and the marketing of wine. Behind the long wall is a highly organised and refined factory process laid out in a rational linear manner. To the roadside of the wall is the sales area with the forms moving away from the functionally derived forms of the rear and reflecting the dynamics of the innovative marketing exercise it will contain. It is a simple structure, distorted and extended, with an impression of the incompleteness to which Warn refers.

The tilt-up concrete slabs of the winery are held apart, as if a propped temporary structure, placing emphasis on the mechanics of their construction and allowing glimpses of the wine making process going on behind. The steel frame extending from the wall of undifferentiated slabs suggests that the line of slabs could be assembled, disassembled, or continued at any time. The front-of-house began as a simple structure and was stretched and then distorted to the point where D+W enjoyed working with the possibility of not being in total control.

To achieve the scale of the grand architectural gesture along the Bussel Highway and to ensure completion of the building to coincide with the next vintage, D+W relinquished any aspiration for refined detailing. The scale and linear form

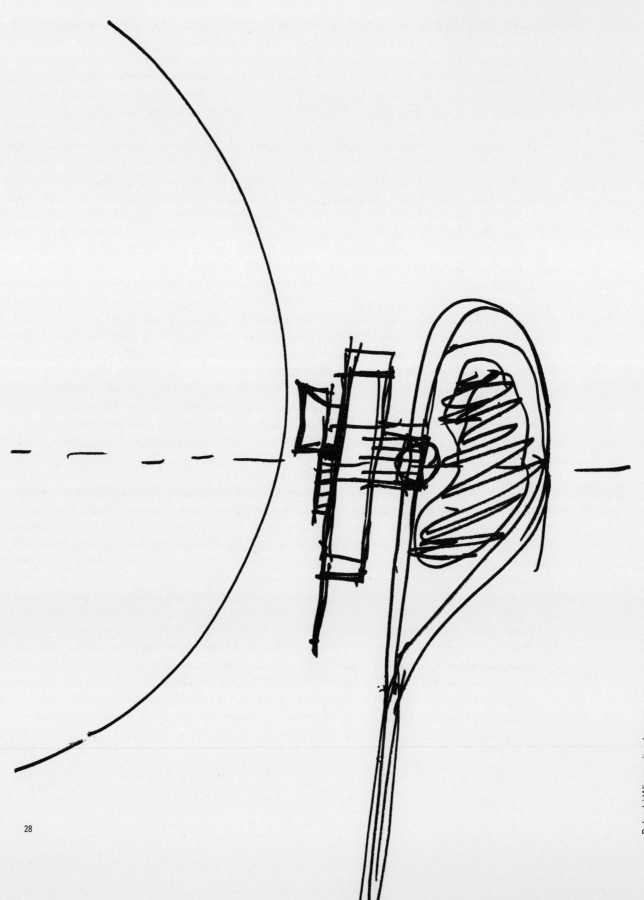

Palandri Winery site plan

allows the building to act as a symbol for the marketing aspect of the project. When completed this will be one of the largest wineries in the rapidly growing premium wine producing area in the south-west of Western Australia.

The grand architectural gesture, rare in Perth, has also been utilised by D+W in the Goddard house. It uses the gesture of the big wall, the monumental rammed limestone wall, containing and protecting the lightweight house behind. If it can be claimed that the development of any material is characteristic of recent Perth architecture, it would be rammed limestone, a local variation of traditional pisé, a material that has about it its own tectonic demands which the architects test in this building. The clarity of the idea of the big thick wall is sustained and made evident within the building, contrasting with the corrugated iron cladding of the other side of the house, the cool south side, with its taut thin neatly detailed surfaces.

The Goddard house is built in Fremantle, an area with significant claims as an important architectural heritage area. As a result, the strong and modern forms of the Goddard house met with considerable opprobrium from the local community. The house was seen as not 'fitting' within a relatively homogeneous area of turn-of-the-century houses and also as a challenge to the local view of what constituted 'home', better represented, it was thought, in the earlier homes surrounding it – with the past, perhaps, seen as a refuge from the present. D+W have faced similar difficulties with the Glick, Chauvel and Lincoln Street houses.

Perhaps because the built heritage of Western Australia is so young, so scant, and so subject to the desire to rebuild, heritage watchers are especially zealous in their protection of the buildings that do remain. In Perth the built heritage is proving to be a difficult and ideologically contentious architectural field.

D+W have not undertaken a great deal of work on heritage buildings. However, when given the chance to take on such work, the practice has demonstrated that it is able to produce bold but essentially respectful relationships between the old and the new in a way that is rare in Western Australia.

Two examples are worthy of mention and they reveal both the difficulties the practice encounters in the field and its capacity to produce innovative hybrids out of the existing buildings and their new insertions.

The redevelopment of the old Claremont Fire Station demonstrates their approach to designing changes to a heritage building when they have a supportive and enthusiastic client. In determining the primary order of the original building they retain the crucial elements and reveal them with greater clarity and emphasis in the completed project. While the room at the rear, with an egg-shaped plan, is a daring insertion of a new form into the old fabric, it actually helps articulate the flanking existing forms. In a cultural climate that is more receptive to replication of the old, the creation of an ersatz tradition, D+W use modern forms, materials, and finishes, clarifying and enhancing the reading of differences between the old and the new. In other instances, not involving the retention of key elements, there are seamless connections between the new and old, such as the way the major rear wall, previously abutting the fire truck garage, was allowed to open completely to the added northern terrace. The complete scheme is not a compromised aggregation of old and new forms but a distinctive new work. The designed additions have extended to the site which now works in a comprehensive manner binding together the disparate elements of building, carpark, signage and landscaping into a new and convincing whole.

The Perth Institute of Contemporary Art [PICA] is accommodated in a conversion carried out by D+W on the old Perth Boys School. The bold interventions initially proposed were refused approval, largely because the building was designed during the last decade of the 19th century, the gold rush period, by George Temple Poole, one of the justifiably revered figures of the Western Australian conservation movement. In spite of major difficulties in obtaining approval to proceed, D+W were able to produce an effective setting for the display of contemporary art which capitalises on the building's initial spatial qualities while inserting a number of critical additions. This included the new stair which strategically reorganises the functional possibilities of the building.

PICA demonstrates how successfully the architects were able to work within substantial constraints imposed by heritage factors. The project also demonstrates their recurring approach to architectural detailing. Detailing assumes a predominant role in D+W's buildings, not just the necessary functional resolution of the working details of a building, but the process and the ethos of detailing which permeates much of the design development and significantly shapes the final product. In some senses all of the details at various scales and complexity are the one detail or the one set of formal and constructional relationships that evolve into a series of permutations and combinations.

In the evolution of a design this detailing process usually springs from the major design and tectonic decisions and develops downwards in scale into the thematically related smaller details. In certain instances, however, this process may evolve upwards, in the reverse order, if the circumstances encourage this.

In the case of PICA the detailing ethos emanates from one of the larger insertions, the new stair, and the formal implications of this major element shape all of the minor details down to the door handles, while also moving upwards in the design process to permeate the design ethos of the overall scheme. The result is that the density and consistency of the detailing makes it possible to convey a sense of thorough reworking of the entire building when in fact only minor interventions have taken place. This approach, where the architecture is largely the product of the process of the detailing contributes a particular flavour to the character of D+W's buildings.

Their detailing moves beyond the domestic whereas many large buildings in Perth are like inflated houses. D+W have always been prepared to engage with materials outside the conventional domestic range and the detailing of their public buildings migrates successfully into their houses.

The Large Animal Facility at The University of Western Australia is, by necessity, a big dumb box of a building but it points towards an architecture that could be. There is a series of architectural gestures that have little to do with the program of housing animals for sophisticated research purposes. The way in which D+W have endeavoured to recess and change the colour of the brickwork to infer vestigial uses like windows and doors suggests the possibility of the ghosts of a building that never was. The heavily worked entrance porches can be regarded as representing D+W's architecture in microcosm, like a little virtuosic Bach fugue. These entrance porches demonstrate the firm's recurring interest in the assembly of a building where various parts that could be enclosed or smudged are aggressively separated – to the point where, in some of their recent buildings, it's almost obsessive. It's as if articulation is one of their mantras: each part needs to be identified, studied and redesigned; each component has an individual identity and integrity. This process results in an architecture of assemblage, working with an assumption that a collection of parts will make a whole: every aspect of a building is reduced to parts, or clusters of parts, and these elements, which mostly evolved from functional necessity, are then used in terms of their potential for formal expression.

Nowhere is this more evident than at the Ballajura Community College. This is the D+W office method at its most resolute: a situation where the planning, when reduced in scale becomes the details and the details enlarged become the site plan, the plan, the elevations, or the sections. This recent work is revealing of the importance and the longevity of the tendency to systematise in D+W's work. Partly this is the result of the project's program that calls for a systematic and repeated organization of spatial units: a task that suggests a constructional system as a possible generator of the design and in this case a system that places particular emphasis on the technological aspects of construction: again, it is an architecture of assemblage.

This building is a faithful outcome of the diagrams produced by the office: the school is a mechanism to educate and the school design is very mechanistic, like the anatomical dissection, beguilingly exploded and exposed. It is a project with enormous clarity and with considerable authority.

Even though the Ballajura Community College is extensively systematised, D+W cannot resist tampering with the comprehensiveness of the system due to their interest in other architectural imperatives and the nature of the building's use. This tendency creates tectonic and formal conflicts and fractures which enrich the buildings and elevate them from the potential banality of systematised diagrams.

Conclusion

Uncompromising vision is a rare characteristic of Perth architecture as is the relentlessness necessary for pushing a project to realise its full potential. D+W have constructed an architectural approach that comes from their acutely considered body of work and from a self-assumed role as the outsiders in an architecturally conservative city. They have a consistent rhetoric about what they're doing, what they intend doing and what they've done. This has allowed them to maintain an exacting quality in their work while also pursuing the idea of making things better through the evolving experiment.

Dick Donaldson claims that the partnership 'will maintain a medium sized studio-based design practice and will continue to resist becoming a corporate office.' He sees an inevitable universalising but tempered by a concern for maintaining cultural differences:

"Global acceptance and desire for new technologies will provide similar technical solutions to common issues, however it is important to maintain and develop cultural and regional influences to provide a sense of place and identity." [11]

Whether the architecture of D+W is created out of a resistance to or a positive response to local particularities, the mark of the place is indelibly set on their work. After fifteen years of architectural partnership in the city of Perth they leave no doubt that theirs is a continuing project which will, by its commitment, rigour, and inventiveness, continue to both express and form the culture of the place.

Geoffrey London
Duncan Richards

1   Simon Leys, 'The Paradox of Provincialism' in The Angel & the Octopus, Duffy and Snellgrove, Sydney, 1999, p. 279.
2   Geoffrey Warn, Donaldson + Warn: 'Playing on the Wing of Pragmatism', Royal Melbourne Institute of Technology, Masters by Project, 1999, p. 5.
3   Simon Leys, 'The Angel & the Octopus', Duffy and Snellgrove, Sydney, 1999, p. 278.
4   Reyner Banham, Los Angeles: 'The Architecture of Four Ecologies', 1971.
5   For a full discussion of the appreciation of the Eames by the Smithsons, see Alison and Peter Smithson, 'Changing the Art of Inhabitation', Artemis, London, 1994, pp. 71-105.
6   Ibid., p. 85.
7   Geoffrey Warn, Donaldson + Warn: 'Playing on the Wing of Pragmatism', p. 51.
8   Dick Donaldson, interview with Geoffrey London, 7 June 2000.
9   Geoffrey Warn, Donaldson + Warn: 'Playing on the Wing of Pragmatism', p. 59.
10 Geoffrey Warn, Donaldson + Warn: 'Playing on the Wing of Pragmatism', p. 5.
11 Dick Donaldson, interview with Geoffrey London, 7 June 2000.

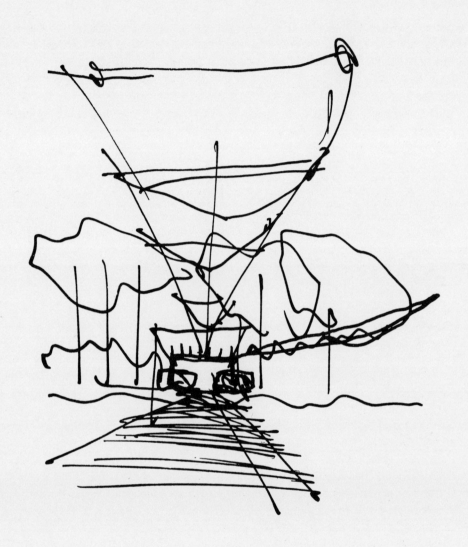

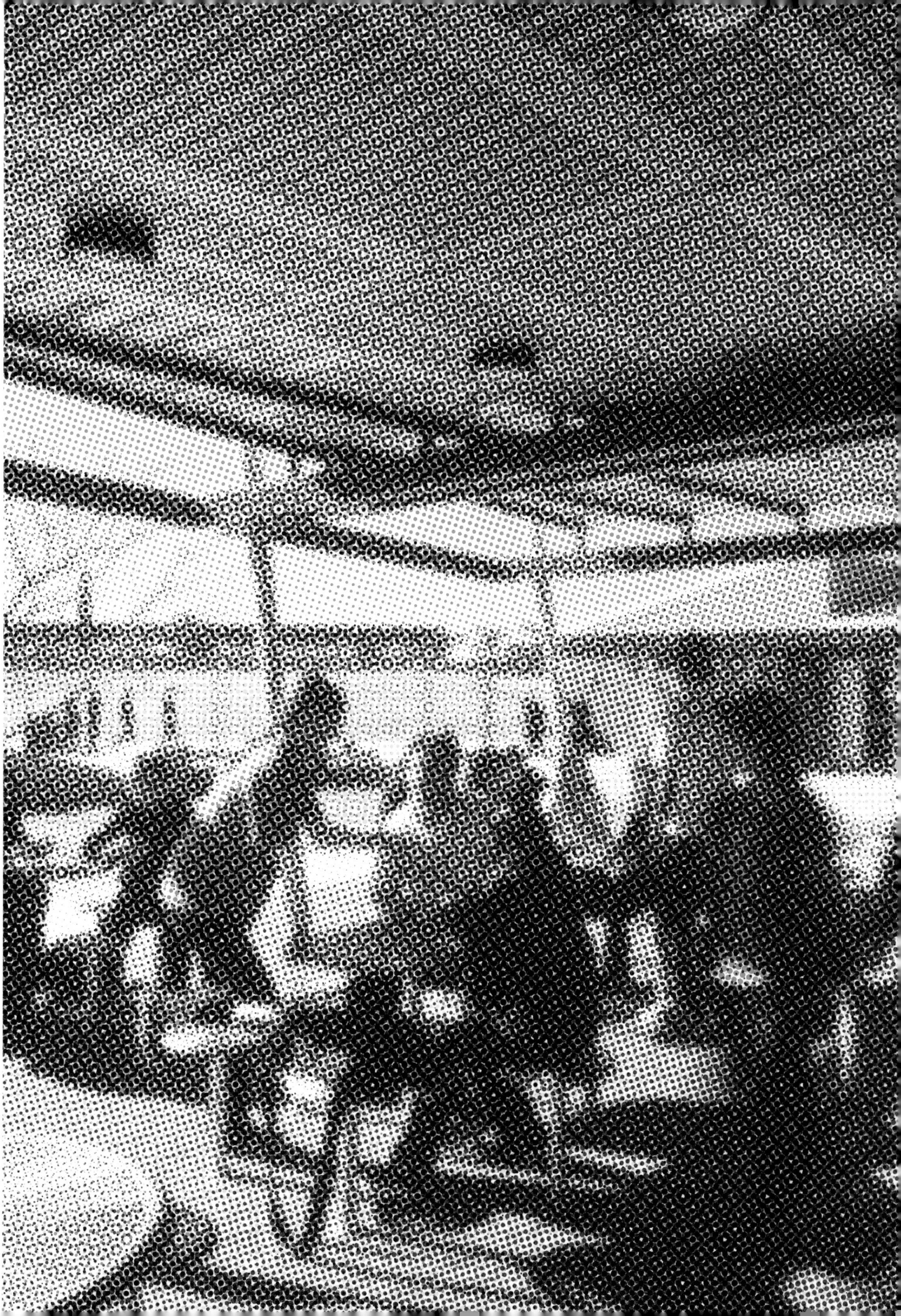

Street façade

Located in a seaside suburb of Perth the two-storey home is designed with a distinct beach-house character. ✚ The standard schedule of domestic accommodation is configured in two halves, placed on either side of a central corridor that stretches from front to rear. The planning is informal with open spacious areas composed around a central courtyard. This courtyard is a focal point in the planning arrangement and allows the northern light into the hub of the house. To maximise the integration of indoor with outdoor spaces, the main living & dining spaces are connected to the courtyard by large sliding glass doors. The light and fresh air that floods the interior can be filtered through louvres, screens, mechanical blinds and vegetation. The interior is clean and crisp. Flush surfaces, combined with full height openings maintain a continuous flow of internal spaces. The simple internal forms are articulated by the light qualities, and the plain surfaces act as a backdrop to the client's various artworks. ✚ Heavy materials and lightweight construction are combined. Half of the house is constructed from an exposed steel frame clad externally with western red cedar siding. This lightweight construction envelopes the larger open and flexible areas; the living, sleeping and dining spaces. Load bearing concrete block construction is used for the service spaces, kitchen, wet areas, store rooms and staircases.

Tasmanian Oak flooring is used throughout to give the activity and circulation spaces a warm, haptic and visual unity. ✚ Contained and compressed spaces, tall double height volumes, expansive glazed areas and an easy flow between inside & outside help to give a variety of experiences that are continuously changing with the cycles of weather and season. The exposed natural finishes of the timber siding and blockwork are gradually being marked by weather to give the house's geometric form a beautiful and varied patina.

North

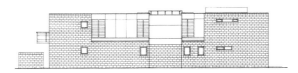

West

South

East

First floor gallery

Above: View from courtyard. Meals area and vaultec ceiling beyond.   Facing page: Cottesloe street.

Glendinning Residence, view from the beach

Glendinning Residence

City Beach, Western Australia

This house is located on the edge of a seaside suburb that meets the Indian Ocean. ✦ A wedge shaped sloping site, with spectacular ocean views across the narrow boundary of the site, suggested a juxtaposition of a long thin lightweight element against a rectangular solid form, which together enclose an external outdoor space. ✦ The project presents two distinct facades in response to the different site aspects; a suburban street façade and an ocean façade. The solid nature of the street façade and its formal address is consistent with the surrounding masonry houses. The ocean façade presents a different set of constraints and opportunities. The design resolves the conflict of expansive west facing views and the resulting heat gain by minimising glazing to the west and maximising outlook from the north elevation. ✦ The primary circulation space has been designed to provide continuous contact with the ocean views when moving around the house. The balcony and external stair detail exhibits a nautical character.

42

North elevation

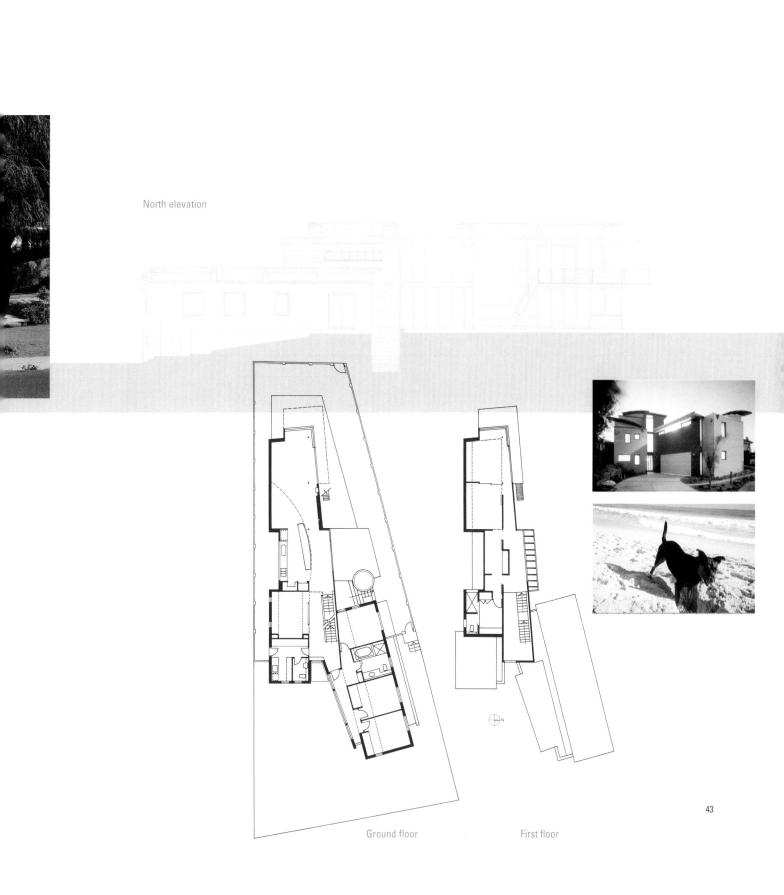

Ground floor   First floor

43

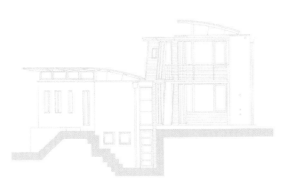
West elevation

44

Above: ANZ West Perth, courtyard. Below: Detail of sun screens. Facing page: ANZ Morley, entry façade and canopy.

ANZ Bank and Offices

West Perth & Morley, Western Australia

A series of commercial bank and office developments addressing urban and environmental issues and maximising each site's development potential have been carried out for the Australia and New Zealand Banking Group. The projects integrate the ANZ corporate image and contemporary approach to design. ✛ The West Perth project responds to the City's intentions for the future streetscape and urban development of the area. By occupying the full extent of the site boundary the integrity of the street is maintained and a positive end definition to the urban block is achieved. An articulated steel screen defines a covered public pedestrian access along the western elevation and also serves to create an identifiable entry court to the first floor offices. In response to environmental conditions, this screen also incorporates sun and wind sensitive electrically operated external sun shading blinds. ✛ At the Morley project, the program provided an opportunity for a double height space to the banking chamber, providing a pleasant aspect for the first floor offices to overlook the large interior space. The east elevation incorporates steel sun shade canopies and electrically operated external blinds to reduce glare and minimise heat load to the banking chamber. The design utilises precast concrete wall and floor panels for economy and to maintain a tight construction period. The central elliptical support column to the canopies is specially designed and fabricated from structural aluminium.

Above: ANZ West Perth, automatic sun shading blinds within steel framed colonnade along western façade

Right: ANZ Morley, street elevation

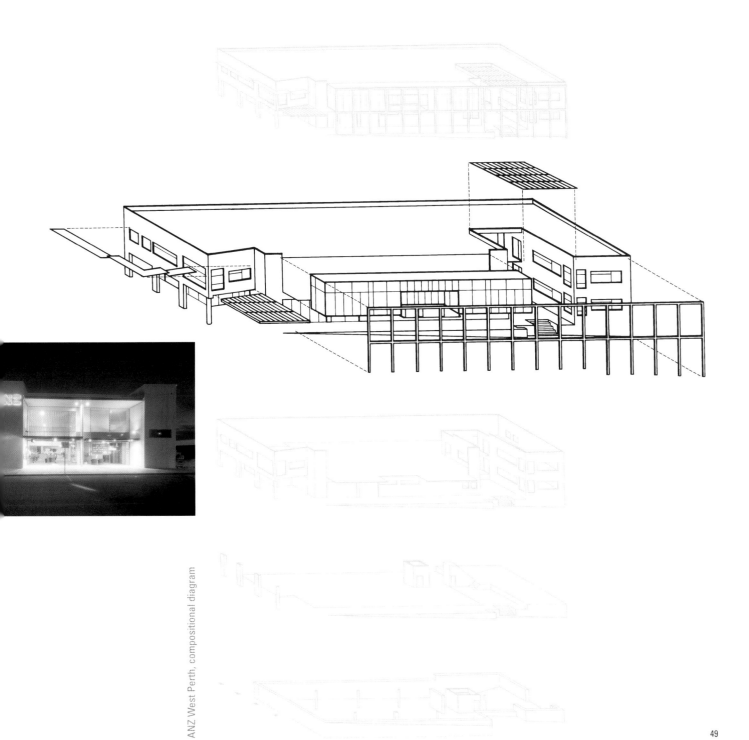

ANZ West Perth, compositional diagram

In the evolution of a

usually springs

from the   major design

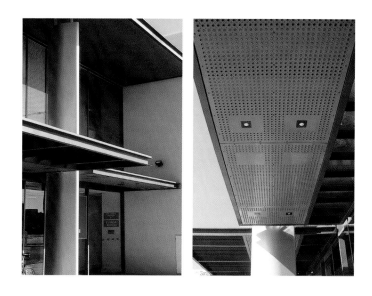

and tectonic decisions

and develops downwards

in scale

design the detailing process

Facing page: ANZ Morley, details of entry canopy. Below: ANZ West Perth, corner details

into the smaller
details

Tingle Shelter in the Valley of the Giants forest

Left: Truss spanning the creek below. Right: Guyed pylon supporting trusses. Facing page: Early study models.

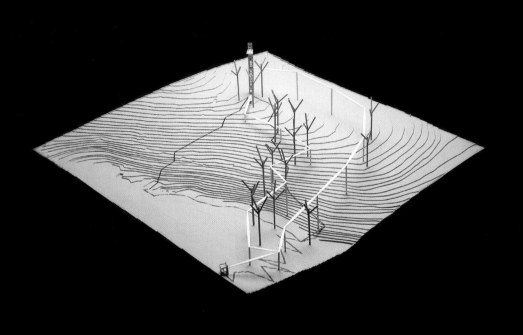
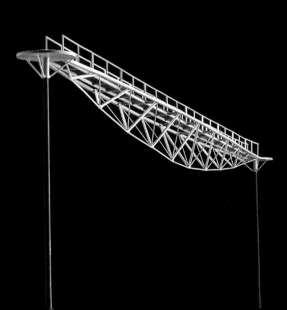

This competition winning submission offered us the opportunity to try an intensely collaborative design process by inviting artist David Jones and structural engineer Adrian Roberts to the project team. ✦ This project held a dense matrix of challenges and issues; environmental, experiential, educational, economic, political, aesthetic, historical, cultural. The focus was on an old tourist destination within a national reserve, the site of some of the planet's oldest trees. Tingle trees are a species of eucalypt wholly unique to this part of the world. The client, a State government department responsible in part for forest management, was looking for an educational spectacle that would attract more visitors to this unique forest, reduce damage to the sensitive eco-system caused by an increase in tourists, and yield a substantial economic return for a relatively low capital commitment. ✦ Our solution proposed 60 metre long trusses threaded through the forest, gradually ascending to the tree canopies to offer commanding views over the ancient forest and out to the distant landscape. The entire journey is accessible to visitors in wheelchairs.

Above: Engineer and architect plotting onto the surveyors map a path for the walkway.

Tingle Shelter

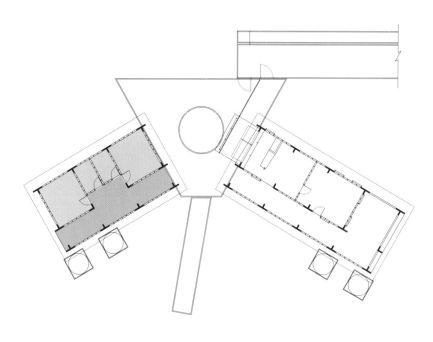

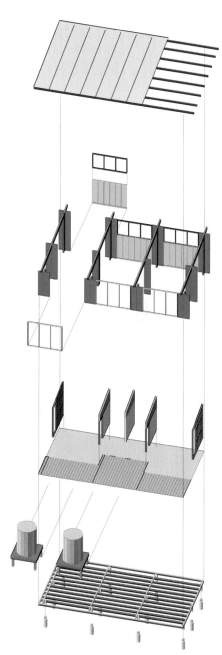

Tingle Shelter system and elements diagram

metal sheeting

rain water tank

purlin

beam

stud frame wall

stud frame

boxed column

floor overlay

jarrah decking

Rain water catchment

Orientation deck and Tingle Shelter

Detailing of the trusses was kept simple to minimise fabrication and assembly costs. Walkway elements were kept short to suit bulk transport to the remote site and to enable easy, low impact erection of the large structure in the forest. The trusses are supported on tubes fabricated from cor-ten steel sheet. These pylons are coloured and scaled to the tree trunks while the silver coloured galvanised members of the trusses resemble the silvery grey tones of the tree top branches. ✛ Like the sky walk, the Tingle shelter also employs modular construction, enabling both features to be expanded, should this be required by future demands. The scale of this small building was exaggerated vertically and the addition of verandahs and covered decks helps the structure command some visual presence amongst the massive trees and dense undergrowth. ✛ The walkway intentionally sways with the movement of the visitors, reminiscent of a child's tree-house. Reaching a height of around 45 metres above the forest floor, each visitor can truly experience the canopies of these giant and ancient trees. ✛ Since its opening the development has been a resounding success, visited by millions of tourists and generating surplus income despite the modest entry fee.

Plan and diagrammatic section

Defining a tight construction site to minimise damage to the forest floor. Following page: The highest spans crossing the creek below provide views of the forest and out to the distant ranges.

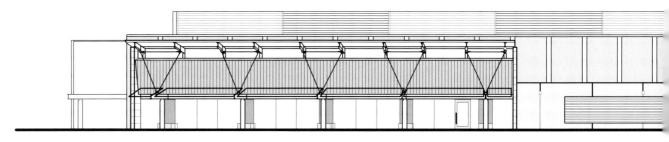

West

South

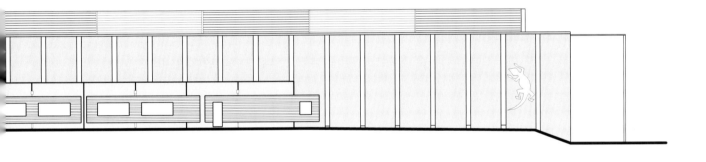

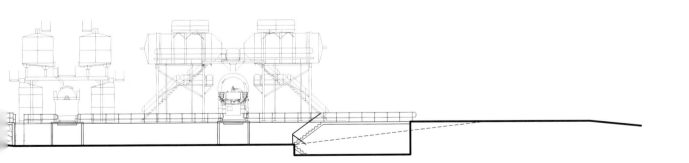

Facing page (above): Structural elements located outside the building enclosure; (below): Flying canopies on northern façade of sales and display building.

Palandri Winery

Margaret River, Western Australia

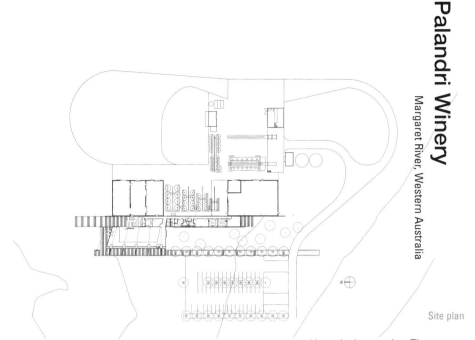

Site plan

For the Margaret River region of Western Australia this is one of the larger wineries constructed in a single exercise. The current 1500 tonne crushing capacity can be increased to over double that quantity without alterations to the building fabric. And, a further requirement: the winery needed to be completed in breakneck speed to meet the first vintage. Additional to these demands our challenge was to test if an architectural experience could be captured by low budget materials put together with basic construction methods. We utilised unfinished tilt-slab concrete panels and a simple steel portal frame shed structure clad with off-the-shelf insulated coolroom panels and pre-painted profiled steel sheet roofing. The winery's production processes of delivery, crushing, waste removal, pressing, fermenting, maturing, storing, bottling and dispensing etc. are organised behind the long concrete panel wall. On the public side of this wall are the laboratories and staff facilities plus an attached building dedicated to the promotion, sales and enjoyment of wine. This building blends the industrial language of the winery with an aesthetic more often found in contemporary cafes and retail environments. The logic of construction, production and economics used for the winery is distorted and disengaged when brought to the sales and display area, resulting in a splayed structural grid and the overt visual expression of the building's tension and compression – forces that are commonly resolved in columns within the building's skin, or a load bearing wall. The interior is rich in colour and texture. Wine and associated merchandise is displayed on units which can be re-arranged in a wide variety of configurations. The sales and display area opens out to a sunny terrace and garden on the northern side, providing outdoor seating under a shade canopy which is supported off a structural bay located outside the enclosing walls. The terrace is linked to the interior via a small cafe and wine tasting area, both with views across the rural landscape. ✚ Unlike the majority of wineries in the region, the Palandri winery elects not to call upon a rustic aesthetic or a traditional building style to lend credibility to its produce, preferring an image that confidently conveys the spirit of a relatively new local industry that is gaining an international reputation for its wine.

Study model

Following page: Western façade, concrete panel concealing tank farm

Left: Wine tasting counter. Centre: Interior sales display area. Right: Tank farm and work area. Facing page: North-western corner of sales and display building.

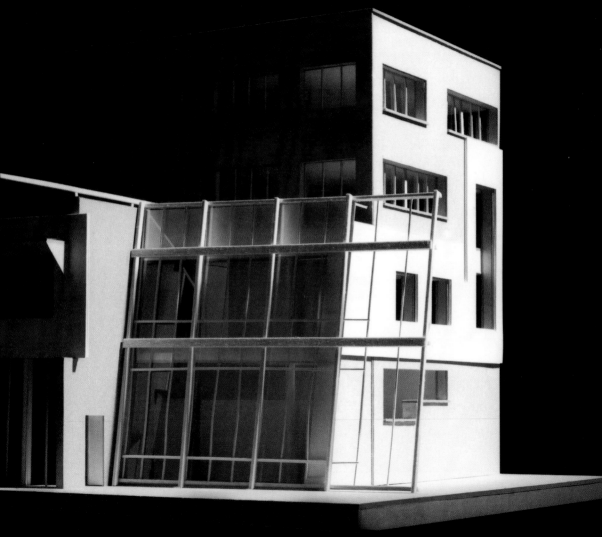

eytesbury Headquarters

East Perth, Western Australia

A commission to design the new headquarters for an exciting company, a family business with vast land holdings, a beef export business, a transport firm, vineyards and a winery, a chain of international theatres, thoroughbred racehorses, a vintage car collection, a major private art collection and one of the nation's leading construction companies. ✚ The scheme mixed a public art gallery, café / restaurant, underground parking, staff accommodation and a wide variety of general working and meeting spaces, all overlooking the Swan River and a recently formed inlet. Although the project did not proceed beyond the design stage, a great deal of fun was had exploring, with the client group, options for what would have been a unique and inspiring working environment for this richly diverse company and a model of accommodation for other local corporations.

View from the south-east showing rooftop plant and ducts on the southern façade.   Facing page: Entry canopy and service ducts on northern façade.

LARGE ANIMAL FACILITY

This highly specialised and complex educational facility is densely compacted with building services, equipment and special features developed to support research associated with large animals; mainly sheep and pigs. The building contains several animal holding areas which can be individually climate controlled, plus food preparation and storage areas, all with internal wash down capacity. Also included are staff facilities, offices, medical laboratories, procedures laboratories, a post-mortem room and, for highly specialised perinatal research, a fully equipped surgical operating suite that is optically linked to student training areas. The building integrates a purpose designed waste removal system that improves operating efficiency. This energy-hungry building is equipped with several other technical features to minimise energy consumption. ✛ Although the building's form is closely allied to the Campuses' dominant aesthetic style and palette of materials, there are several idiosyncrasies particular to this project. The organisation of this building's functions is tightly bound to its operational demands. The visual composition of the main facades responds accordingly. The conventional expression of a regular structural frame and related window pattern has been subjected to the practical logic and preferences of the services engineers. The long elevations are dominated by vertical ducts which envelope mechanical risers, pipes and cables connected to the full length rooftop plant room, making the initial services installation easier and future repairs and upgrades much less of a disruption. These external ducts are of differing widths and do not relate to the almost regular structural grid. The few required windows occur where the users wanted them. The resulting facades appear both symetrical and asymetrical and the solid mass of the basic form seems visually loosened and paired open by the expressed detailing.

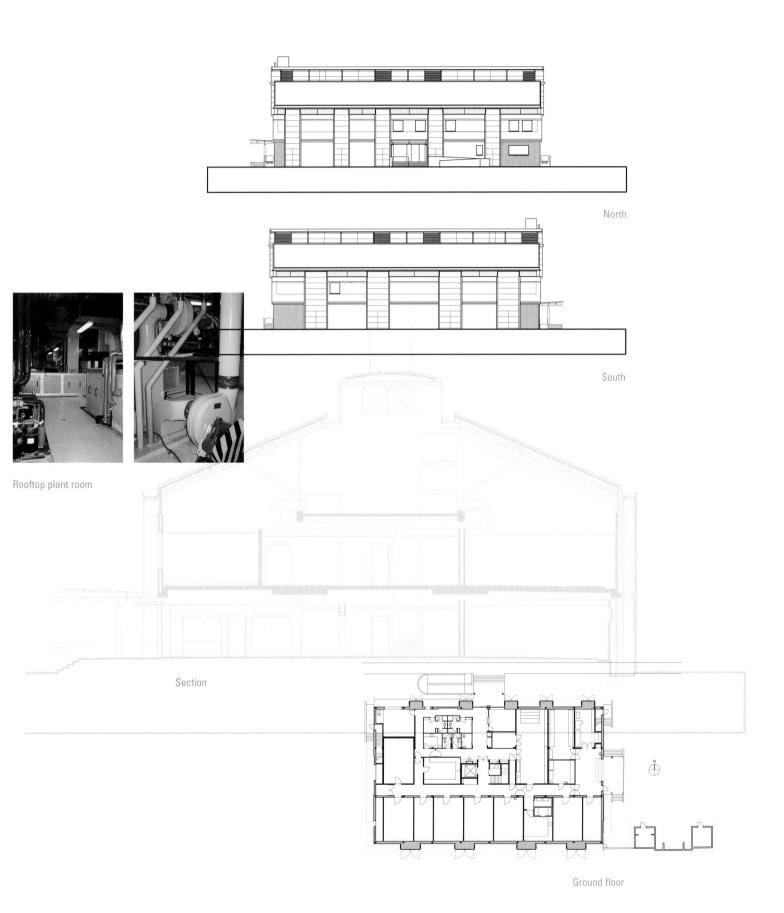

North

South

Rooftop plant room

Section

Ground floor

the   ghost of a

building that never was

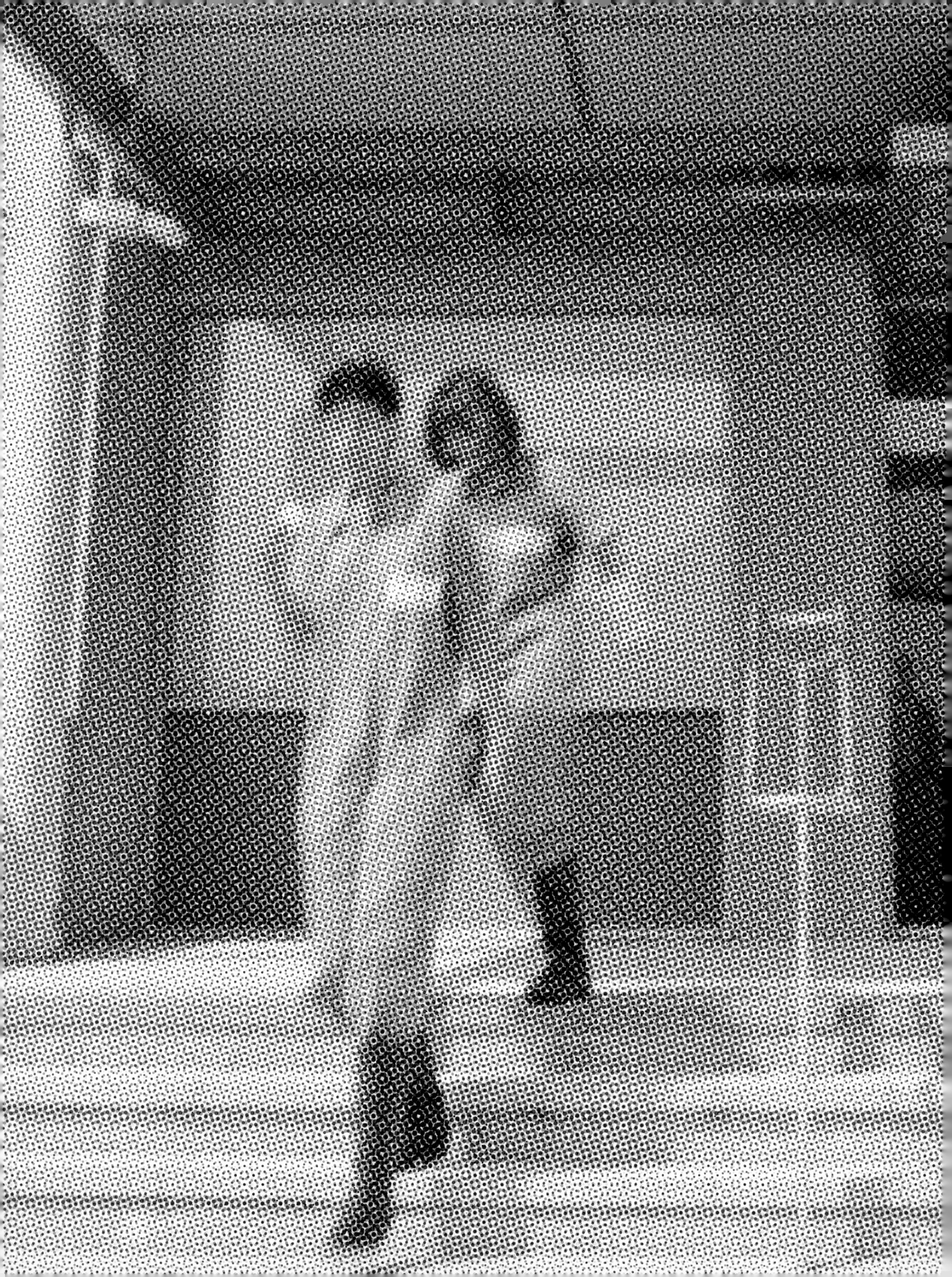

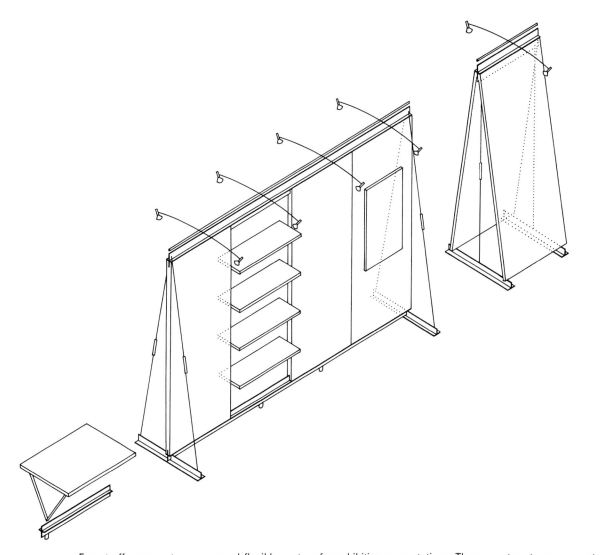

Exsyst offers a contemporary and flexible system for exhibition presentations. The current system represents several years of research and development of prototypes. The design demonstrates potential to be developed into a sophisticated system by the application of contemporary fabrication technology. ✚ Its main features include: lightweight hollowcore panels and aluminium rails, rapid erection, fully integrated lighting system, featuring unobtrusive low voltage dichroic lamps, double sided free standing display panels without awkward corners or stabilisers. The system has the ability to display a wide variety of items with the addition of integrated components including a hanging system, display shelving and tables.

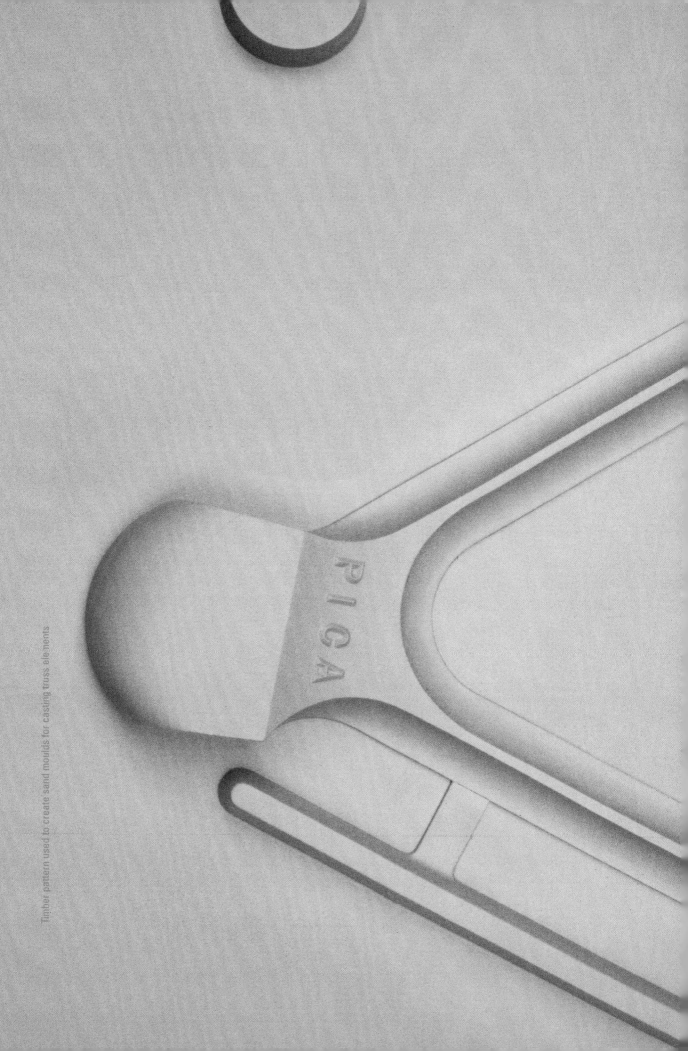

Timber pattern used to create sand moulds for casting truss elements

Ductile-iron castings used for structural support trusses over performance space

Perth Institute of Contemporary Arts

Perth Cultural Centre

New staircase

This heritage listed building was constructed during the late 1890s as a Boys School. Our commission was to adapt the building for the newly formed contemporary arts institution (PICA) while maintaining the integrity of the original architecture. Initially, more radical designs were explored on the pathway to the final solution. These earlier designs were rejected mostly for reasons of budget or heritage. ✚ In the commissioned scheme the building's original circulation routes have been modified to create gallery spaces leading off the large central hall. A new foyer and staircase provides access to the ground floor and upper level galleries.

A performance space was created on the lower level. Bow trusses, designed with small cast iron elements, were assembled within the building and positioned to support the upper gallery floor. Assembling the trusses within the building was the preferred option over demolishing part of the façades to introduce the construction equipment and larger structural members required to achieve the open, column free space. A small public café was also included on the ground floor, plus a members' resource room, storage and administration facilities on the upper level. ✚ Earlier proposals to include a media workshop, performers dressing rooms and prop stores, library and research areas and a bridge to the nearby city carpark were postponed until a later stage of development.

Early model showing proposal for central performance space and pedestrian bridge from carpark to PICA's first floor

Stair detail

Central gallery with installation by Japanese artist Goji Hamarda. Facing page: Casting, testing and installing ductile iron truss members.

Perth Foreshore Competition, concept diagram of the city's growth to the river and development sketch of ferry terminal at river edge

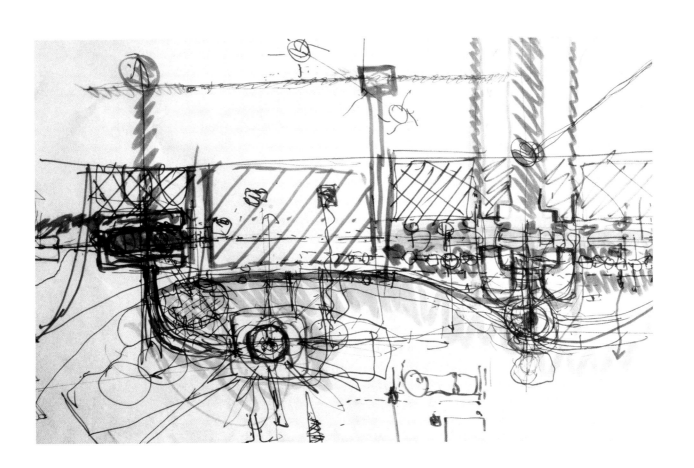

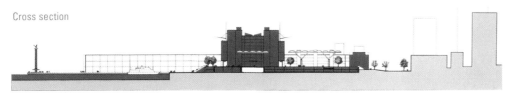

Cross section

Facing page: Diagrammatic model of the future city seen from the east. Above: Axonometric of civic square and city garden.

During the early 1990s several factors prompted a reconsideration of the image and quality of the city centre: a gradually increasing state population, a noticeable increase in vehicular traffic, a decline in the number of local residents, competition between businesses, relocation of city's institutions, greater acknowledgment of the economic and cultural benefits of tourism and media attention given to a citizens action group who were calling for a better capital city. Under such a review the structural problems of the city plan became evident. In response, the city government hosted an international design competition for the beautification of the city's most picturesque edge – that which is frequently featured on postcards and television promos. The call of the brief was to link the city to its water, the Swan River. But we felt the competition organizer's vision avoided the more difficult questions and challenges: those concerned with urban growth, urban living, public transport, sustainable development, an uninspiring urban environment and the growing trend to decentralise almost everything from the city to the suburbs. ✚ Rather than embark upon a few kilometres of stylistic planting, we felt a long term masterplan strategy, realised in progressive stages, was needed to reconnect the city to its river and to encourage Perth's transformation from what is becoming an architecturally generic modern city back to a unique city. Our design proposed two fingers of urban development be extended to the edge of the Swan River, one commercial and civic, the other predominantly residential. The western finger would link the existing cultural centre on the northern side of the city to a new civic and entertainment complex beside the water. This finger embraces the city's established pedestrian pathways, extending these from the train station through commercial towers and retail malls to the waterside civic complex which would contain State and City government offices, a city hall and a large urban plaza. New retail and entertainment facilities would help rejuvenate city life, keeping it alive well beyond the conventional working day and week. The integration of a redeveloped ferry port would provide greater access to the city from the water. ✚ The eastern finger of development extends an urban residential district to the river. Apartments and town houses located above retail strips flank both sides of a long green park. The linear park connects an existing educational college on the northern edge of the city to a new waterside market place and public jetties on the river. A light rail service runs through the green spine and across to the new civic plaza, bringing city residents and tourists using this mode of transport into the civic heart of the city. Their journey would pass through Perth's beautiful historic gardens, with its early judicial architecture, and past a potentially expanded performing arts centre, the passengers always in view of the Swan River and the city skyline.

Stage 1

Stage 2

Stage 3

Stage 4

It

showed the potential
for an achievable urbanity

and, importantly, a fruitful
relationship   between
built form and

nature

West elevation

The brief for the WA Maritime Museum called for a large-scale public edifice of landmark status, to be sited in the harbour, designed in the 1890s by the engineer C.Y. O'Connor, at the mouth of the Swan River. The once historic and busy port is now much less used and facing major redevelopment. Its signature piece will be a new maritime museum, to display the internationally prized racing yacht Australia II beside numerous sailing craft, a large collection of maritime memorabilia and artifacts and a WWII Ovens Class submarine. ✚ Our design for the building employs a large, enveloping shell that folds out to the west. Propping the shell off the wharf on angled struts enables visitors to gaze over the harbour and out to the vast horizon of the Indian Ocean, in a gesture intended to stimulate imaginative links between land and sea, past and present. ✚ In visual and formal terms, our museum design is set in contrast with its immediate setting. The project uses the device of a design metaphor to provoke an architectural form that references certain physical and emotional features of the context. By abstractly echoing local forms, materials, colours and textures – such as ships' hulls, sails, the scale of the dockland's industrial machinery – we have endeavoured to give the design a degree of familiarity and so promote wider accessibility to contemporary design. ✚ In minimising the impact of construction, the project endeavours to utilise the best features of the site. The museum brief is spread into existing and under-utilised industrial sheds, to reduce the scale of the new building and retain the character of a working port. Site planning also maintains the public's free and easy access to the water's edge. The museum is located directly adjacent to the old slipyards, with the submarine displayed on a slip constructed during WWII to service such vessels. This gesture embraces the old slipyard as an outdoor museum and places the submarine in an appropriate historical context. That siting decision, and the strategy for forming the building, allow the crucial site-lines from the harbour master's observation point atop the Fremantle Port Authority's administration tower. ✚ Light also generated our design, which invites views into and through the museum (from several positions, including the Roundhouse). Filtered light streams through the skin of the shell, while natural light is regulated into some of the galleries; others use artificial light. Translucent and coloured glass, nylon sailcloth and perforated metal sheeting filter and modify the strong light in a variety of ways. Other themes, such as 'loose-fit design', 'ambulation' and 'captured space', further elaborate the design strategy.

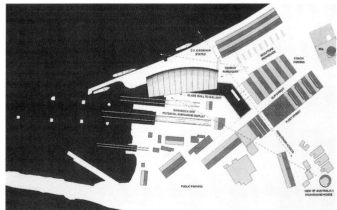

Site plan

* in conjunction with Hassell Pty Ltd.

Facing page: Concept model, view from the entry into the display galleries

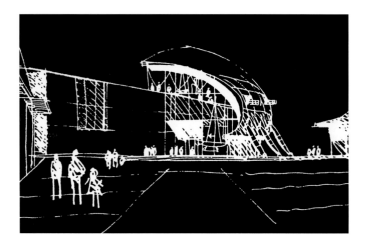

Early sketch: The approach to the main entry

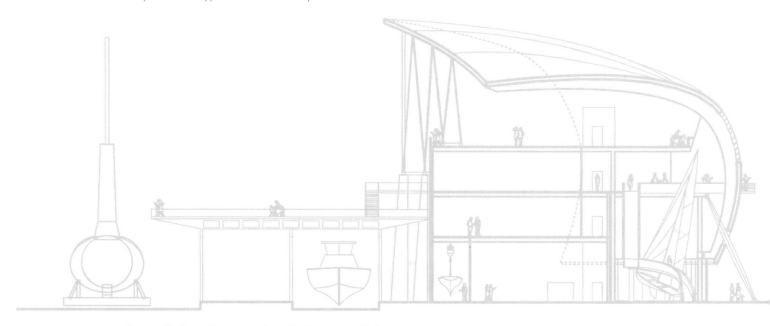

Section: The Ovens Class submarine is displayed on an old slipway

Computer image of the gallery shell superimposed onto a photograph of the Harbour's sheds and wharf machinery

Computer image of the Australia II gallery seen from the Indian Ocean

Colour identifies building types and functions

Ballajura Community College

Ballajura, Western Australia

Entry statement

A new senior school, with the potential to be relocated in the future, was the third stage of development at Ballajura Community College. The purpose for embarking on the idea of a relocatable school, in this new subdivision of Perth, came from the challenge to address the economic ramifications associated with the typical initial peak and gradual decline of student enrolments, as the local population matures. This results in the school development being under-utilised over a twenty year period. ✛ Careful consideration has been taken to integrate the building forms and landscape, with particular attention to provide people orientated spaces between the buildings. The scale, massing, colours and details of buildings and the spaces between buildings have been designed to liven both the external and internal spaces, assist in the legibility of building types and functions, and provide the school with an individual identity and spirit. ✛ Each building provides variety of visual character by utilising distinctive forms, bold use of colour, texture and a variety of standard materials. The relocatable construction system is centred on a modular and uniformly detailed approach utilising industry accepted construction standards. It emphasises the modular nature of the design through a palette of standard components and wall panels. ✛ School elements have been organised to promote clear definition of entries and functional relationships within and between spaces. ✛ To support the senior school curriculum and provide for a variety of teaching methods, different learning area sizes, seminar rooms and support areas combined with non-dedicated learning areas for flexibility of room usage, and computer resource areas to encourage self-directed learning, have been incorporated into the design.

Site plan: Development stages

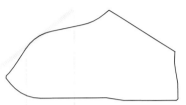
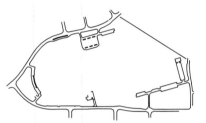

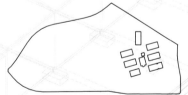

Above: Visual arts building viewed across sunken courtyard

Below: Typical circulation zone incorporating computer resource areas adjacent to learning areas

Site plan

Above: Visual arts building. Right: View across court to general learning area beyond.

Facing page: Extended shade structure and seating contains the external courtyard and provides the basis for future addition, change or adaption.

View of meeting room 'egg' from the courtyard

Claremont Fire Station Conversion

Claremont, Western Australia

This heritage listed building is a significant local landmark on a major arterial road connecting Perth to the port city of Fremantle. The building required extensive modifications to adapt the old Fire Station to its new use as a café, office and apartment complex. The new functions bring the public back to a building which was previously an after hours meeting and dance hall venue for the developing local community. ✦ The main central space, once the engine room, has become the restaurant and bar. The service areas and a private dining room are accommodated in the two flanking wings. Office accommodation and a single apartment are located on the first floor, each with a separate entry at ground level. Opening up the centre of the building to the unused area at the rear of the site provides a sunny landscaped aspect and contained courtyard. The rear glass doors fold fully open to provide an extension of the interior to the outdoor court. ✦ The design strategy contrasts bold, contemporary elements with the existing heritage architecture. There was a desire to conserve and maintain the existing fabric of the building with new work clearly differentiated from existing, resulting in an exciting marriage of old and new. Where previously existing walls were reinstated they were constructed of brick, and where new walls were introduced, lightweight construction was used. New openings are clearly indicated by steel framing. Other new elements sit as insertions, contrasting with the original building fabric. The first floor conference room 'egg' floats within the extended two-storey volume and spatially connects the ground and first floors. ✦ The café interior was treated in a similar manner where new elements are clearly differentiated from the original fabric. The stainless steel bar, with blue glass and timber attachments, is a focus in the space as it sits beneath the edge of the oval ceiling above.

Entrance canopy and sign   Mezzanine

First floor plan

Underside of the 'egg', as seen from ground floor

Ground foor plan

⊕ N

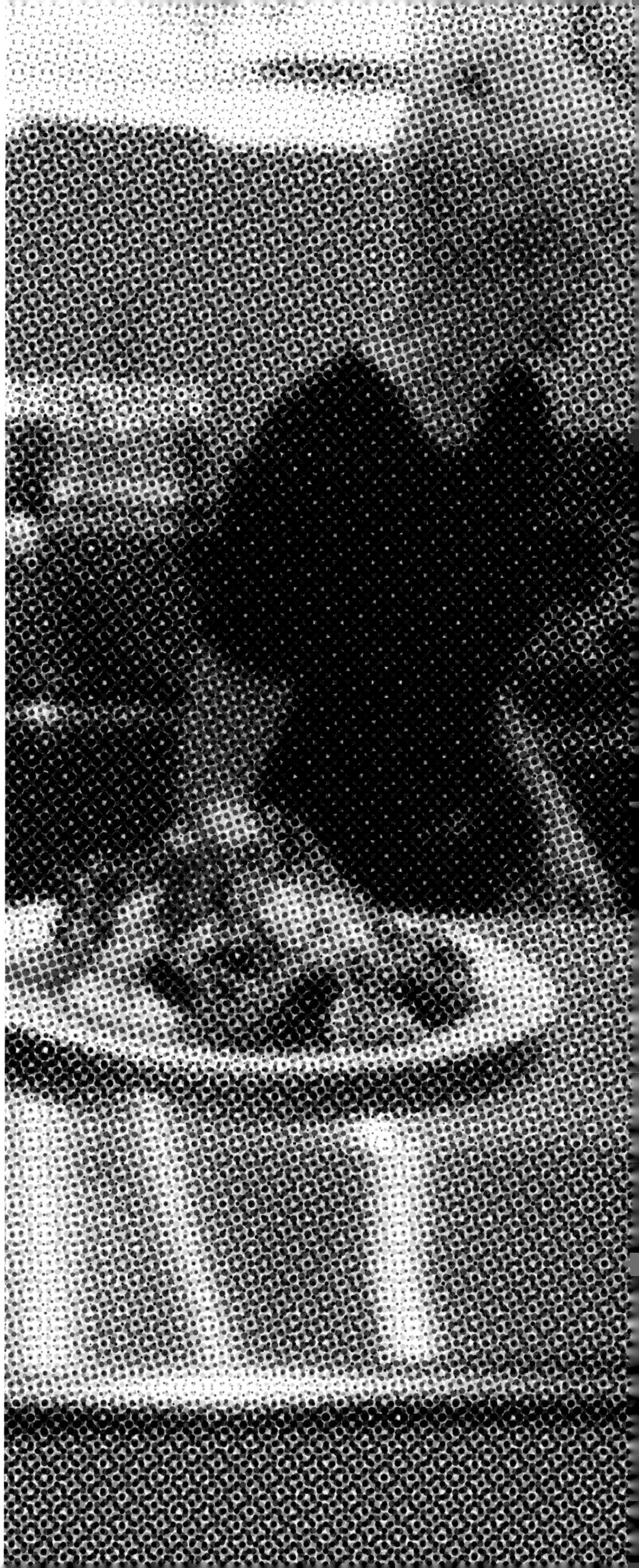

Facing page: View from northern courtyard.

Facing page: First floor entry landing and stair to the roof deck.

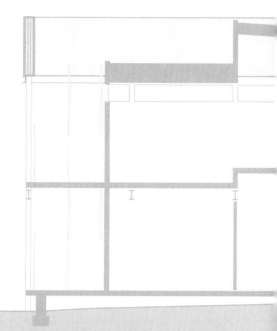

This is one of several projects undertaken with artists or groups involved in the arts. Each has been an absorbing and probing process, working within low budgets and sometimes difficult constraints, but each resulting in a lot to reflect upon. On this occasion the Glick residence was a collaboration with graduate architect Jane Wetherall, artist Rodney Glick and his father Graham, a retired structural engineer. ✛ Glick's interest in a small disused and soon to be demolished foundry was the initiating reference for his new residence and studio situated on a small 90 square metre suburban lot not far from the city centre. Glick's creative work with mundane industrial equipment and products, such as electrical cabinets and security monitors, overlapped the architects'

interests in an aesthetic that is influenced by practical decisions and low cost construction, spoken in the language of modern architecture with a local accent. ✛ The arrangement of domestic elements common to the neighbouring cottages – front porch, compact house, rear patio and workshop/shed in the back yard – are here stacked vertically above the shed, now an artist's studio. The patio, complete with water, light and gas for the bar-b-que, is located on the roof. Contrasts are again prevalent – light and dark, light and heavy, frame and plane, transparent, translucent and opaque, ground deck and roof deck, strip window and boxed windows. An oversized structural frame is expressed externally and left to rust, giving the residence a long but limited life. The external materials and finishes will, over time, become weathered by the strong sun, wind and rain, giving the architecture a distinctly local patina. Via several architectural projects that have considered relationships between structure, skin and contained volume composed with a 'loose formalism', many of the materials and details return us to the initial reference of the small foundry.

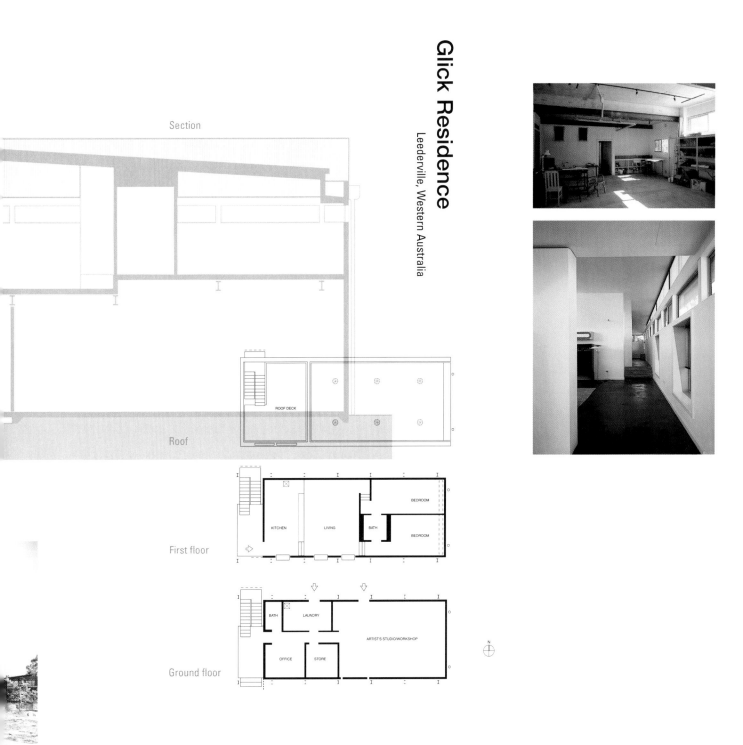

Glick Residence

Leederville, Western Australia

Section

Roof

ROOF DECK

First floor

KITCHEN   LIVING   BATH   BEDROOM

BEDROOM

Ground floor

BATH   LAUNDRY

OFFICE   STORE

ARTIST'S STUDIO/WORKSHOP

N

Facing page: Disused industrial foundry. Right above: Studio on ground floor; (below): View past kitchen and living area to main bedroom

Above: First floor landing and stair to the roof deck. Below (left): Landing detail; (right): Eastern façade. Facing page: Street façade.

Facing page: View across courtyard to dining area at ground level with living area above.   This page: Northern balconies.

The Lincoln Street project is the development of two residential units on a previously single residential site. The duplex demonstrates the development and lifestyle potential of contemporary infill housing in an old inner city subdivision of Perth. The accommodation requirements, room sizes and the layout of the house caters for a variety of occupants and lifestyles. ✛ The courtyard housing model was chosen as it is ideal for the narrow site and its aspect. Dividing the site longitudinally provides a street frontage and rear vehicular access to both units and creates design opportunities for a variety of living spaces with a complimentary outdoor space or view. Each duplex consists of two, two-storey 'pavilions' separated by a central courtyard and connected by a two storey glazed link and first floor bridge. The central courtyard is the locus of the project and was conceived as an outside 'room' contained by a two-storey pergola. It provides a secure and private outdoor living and entertainment space adjacent to the dining area. The courtyard maximises useable outdoor space and capitalises on the narrow northern aspect of the site to capture the sunlight and create a comfortable and spacious quality living environment. ✛ The formal design concept utilises a series of volumes, frames and planar elements to articulate the form in response to the brief, and the site's topographic, urban and environmental conditions.

Above: Upper level living area

Right: Northern façade facing street

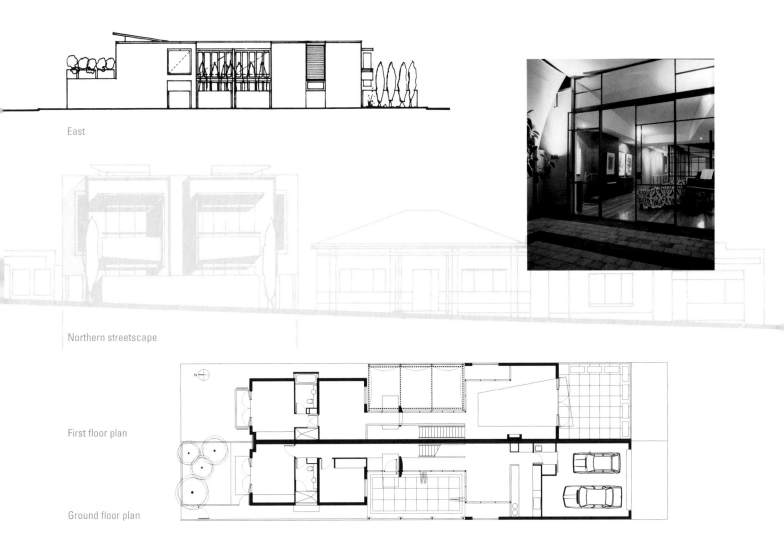

East

Northern streetscape

First floor plan

Ground floor plan

Left: View from upper level looking north across courtyard. Right (above): Courtyard and entry to western dwelling; (below): View from kitchen to courtyard.

There is a of convex space

dominating   sense
rather than concave
opening up   to a vast

Palandri Winery, North façade.

sky

125

DONALDSON + WARN

Awards + Citations		
1990	RAIA (WA): Commendation – Chauvel Residence	
1990	John Flower Fellowship	
1992	RAIA (WA): Commendation – Perth Institute of Contemporary Arts	
1993	Perth Foreshore Competition: AIUS Seminar – Best WA Submission	
1993	University of Western Australia Campus Panel Architect	
1993	Architecture Australia Unbuilt Projects: Urban Design Commendation	
1996	MBA Excellence in Construction Award – Division Four Category Winner: Manjimup Retail Development	
1996	RAIA (WA): Dorma Interior Award, Nexus Drama Facility – Award of Merit	
1996	Western Australian Civic Design Award: Premier's Award, Valley of the Giants Re-development Project	
1996	Western Australian Civic Design Award: Specific Feature Category, Valley of the Giants Re-development Project	
1996	Project Award in Landscape Architecture: Design Category, Valley of the Giants Re-development Project	
1997	RAIA (WA): Civic Design Award, Tree Top Walk and Tingle Shelter – Merit Award	
1997	BHP Australian Steel Award for Architecture, Tree Top Walk and Tingle Shelter	
1997	RAIA, National Architecture Awards: Citation for Access – Tree Top Walk and Tingle Shelter	
1997	Australian Prospectors and Miners Hall of Fame Competition – Commendation	
1998	Urban Development Institute of Australia Awards for Excellence: East Perth Redevelopment Project	
1998	Western Australian Tourism Award: Valley of the Giants Re-development Project	
1998	Western Australian Industry and Export Award: Design Award – Commendation	
1999	RAIA (WA): Multiple Residential Award , Lincoln Street Duplex – Award of Merit	
1999	RAIA (WA): Lincoln Street Duplex – George Temple Poole Award	
1999	Western Australian Tourism Award: Valley of the Giants, Category Winner – Significant Regional Attractions	
1998	AISC Architectural Steel Design Award WA 1999: Relocatable Buildings for Ballajura Community College Senior School	
1999	MBA Excellence in Construction Awards – Best Industrial / Commercial Building: UWA Large Animal Facility	

Exhibitions	
1987	'Aspects of the Unseen', WA Museum. Architectural Drawings
1990	Perth Institute of Contemporary Arts, PICA
1991	Internal Furniture Design, Curtin University
1993	'Altering Architecture', The Door Gallery, Fremantle
1994	Design, Building and Furnishing Exhibition
1995	RAIA WA Chapter Architecture Week, GPO, Perth (Exhibition Curators)
1997	Australian Prospectors and Miners Hall of Fame, Cullity Gallery
1998	International Art Space, Kellerberrin (ASKA)
2000	'Light Houses' Adelaide Festival of Arts, South Australia

Lectures	
1987	'Architectural Jam', Hobart Tas
1987	Sydney University, Sydney NSW
1988	Half Time Club, Melbourne VIC
1988	RMIT, Melbourne VIC
1990	Perth Institute of Contemporary Arts, Perth WA
1991	UCLA, Berkeley, California USA
1992	RMIT, Melbourne VIC
1995	Crossings International, Student Conference, Perth WA
1995	RAIA PD Programme WA Chapter, Perth WA
1995	RAIA PD Programme NSW Chapter, NSW
1995	RMIT, Melbourne VIC
1997	The WEDGE Landscape Conference, Perth WA
1997	RMIT, Melbourne VIC
1999	RAIA PD Programme WA Chapter, Perth WA

Teaching	
1989 – 2000	University of WA, Nedlands WA
1988	RMIT, Melbourne VIC
1982 – 1997	Curtin University, Bentley WA

Donaldson + Warn, Architects

Current Team

Dick Donaldson
Geoff Warn
Sarah Beeck
Janelle Clarke
Mark Giles
Jeremy Feldhusen
Peter Kernot
Jonathon Lake
Debbie Kuh
Angelo Mascuro
Chris Mellor
Robyn Moore
Steven Postmus
Philip Richards
John Sunderland

Web site: http//www.dag@highway1.com.au

Publications

1987	The Architectural Review (February)
1987	Jam Log (Biennial Oceanic Architectural, Education Congress – Hobart)
1988	The Architect (Volume 28 No 2)
1989	Transition – Discourse on Architecture (No 29)
1989	Fremantle Art Review (February)
1990	Architecture Australia (May)
1991	Art Reading Material (ARM) Issue 1, 2 & 3
1991	Art Monthly Australia (November)
1991	The Architect (Volume 31 No 2)
1991	The Architect (Volume 31 No 4)
1991	Internal Furniture Design Brochure
1992	Architecture Australia (February)
1992	Backlogue (April)
1992	Fremantle Art Review (August)
1992	WA Style (September)
1992	The Architect (Volume 32 No 1)
1992	Architecture Australia (May)
1992	Luscombe & Peden; Picturing Architecture
1992	Architecture Bulletin (December)
1992	Art Reading Material (ARM) Issue 8
1993	Architecture Australia (January)
1993	The Architect (Volume 33 No 4)
1993	Monument (Number 1)
1994	Architecture Australia (January/February)
1996	The Architect (Volume 35 No 5)
1996	House and Garden (June)
1996	Trends – Australian Design (Volume 12 No 7)
1996	Landscope (Winter)
1996	Metcalf; Thinking Architecture
1997	Steel Structures (March)
1997	The Architect (Volume 37 No 2)
1997	Monument (Number 18)
1997	The Architect (Volume 37 No 3)
1997	Architecture Australia (November/December)
1997	Australian Prospectors and Miners Hall of Fame, Competition Catalogue
1997	Discovering the Valley of the Giants
1998	Australian New Home Trends (Volume 14 No 12)
1998	Monument (Number 27)
1998	The Architect (Volume 38 No 4)
1998	The Architect (Volume 39 No 1)
1999	The Architectural Review (February)
1999	The Architect (Volume 39 No 3)
1999	AA Architecture: Houses (Issue 18)
1999	Design Trends (Volume 15 No 10)
1999	Steel Profile (Number 68 September)
1999	Monument (Number 32)
2000	Space & Society (Number 88 March)
2000	Stephen Crafti: Beach Houses of Australia & New Zealand, Images Publishing
2001	Jane Amidon: Radical Gardens, Thames and Hudson

Former employees:

Kate Anderson, Mason Arkell, Colin Armstrong, Jane Bennetts, Richard Black, Sandy Bransby, Glen Chamberlain, Chris Chee, Dirk Collins, Matt Crawford, Graham Crist, Andrew Croxon, Bradley Day, Glen De'Franchesch, Jim Dunster, Pia Ednie-Brown, Martyn Hook, Emma Hunt, Ramin Jahromi, Murray Johns, Lincoln Jones, Alison Keys, Graham Kershaw, Aidan Kinsella, Marek Krynski, Mark Langdon, Yong Lee, David Mah, Michael Malinowski, Ian Mathieson, Scott McConn, Lynlee Messenger, Gary Mitchell, Mike Moore, Jeannette Mulachy, Scott Mullen, Tony Naso, Pru O'Connor, Jayne Orton, Trevor Osborne, Stephen Parkin, Finn Pedersen, Simon Pendal, Justin Quinlan, Shaun Robless, Paul Rossen, Glenn Russell, Andrew Scafe, Jill Shelton, William Smart, Teresa Smith, Lee Stickells, Rob Strange, Errol Tout, Andrea Veccia-Scavalli, Dimmity Walker, Kathy Chan, Fiona Walker, Kristy Webb.

Photography Credits (reading from left to right and from top to bottom, im. = image)

Mike Annear :
p.85; p.86 - im.1-2; p.87 - im.1; p.92; p.93 - im. 1-2;
p.94 - im. 3-4-5-7-8-9-10

Leon Bird : Cover; p.9 – Surfer; p.35; p.106; p.107; p.109 - im.1-2-4

Dick Donaldson : p.42 - im.2

Martin Farquharson :
p.6 - im.1; p.10/11; - p.12 - im.1-2; p.13 - im.2; p.16 - im.1-4; p.34/35;
p.36 - im.1-2; p.41; p.42 - im.1; p.43 - im.1; p.44; p.45; p.46; p.47; p.48;
p.49 - im.1-2; p.50 - im.1-2; p.51 - im.1-2; p.52/53; p.54 - im.1-2; p.55;
p.59 - im.1-2; p.67; p.68/69; p.70 - im.1-2-3; p.71; p.72/73; p.75; p.76 -
im.1; p.79; p.80; p.81; p.82 - im.1-2-4; p.96; p.101; p.102; p103 - im.1-2;
p.105; p.108; p.109 - im.3; p.110; p.118; p.119; p.120 - im.1-2;
p.122/123; p.123 - im.1-2; p.24; p.124; p.125

Robert Frith : p.100; p.104 - im. 1-2; p.112; p.113; p.115 - im.1-2; p.116 - im.1; p.117

Rodney Glick : p.114

David Jones : p.56; p.57 - im.1-2-4-5-6-9-10-12; (maquettes); p.61

Ray Leeves : p.39; p.43 - im.2; p.128; Back cover

Gary Sarre : p.37; p.38 - im.1

Ron Tan : p.118; p.121

Geoff Warn :
p.13 - im.1; p.58; p.74; p.76 - im.2; p.77 - im.1-2; p.78; p.79 - sketch;
p.84; p.89 - im.1-6; p.90; p.91; p.94 - im.2; p.97; p.98 - Sketch; p.116 -
im.2-3

D + W, Architects : p.57 - im.3-7-8-11; p.82 - im. 3-5-6

Warn/Leeves : p.5

City of Perth : p.94 - im.1-6-11

Unknown : p.38 - im.2; p.87 - im.2

Satellite Remote Sensing Services, Department of Land Administration, Western Australia.
p.1 - SPOT 4 Multispectral and Pan merged image.
©CNES 1999, ©DOLA 1999.
p.2-3 - Landsat TM, SPOT Pan and DEM merged image.
©ACRES, ©CNES, ©DOLA.

THE UNIVERSITY OF WESTERN AUSTRALIA

The State of Western Australia has made an
investment in this project through ArtsWA in
association with the Lotteries Commission.